IT TAKES MORE THAN A ROOF

MERCY HOUSING'S MISSION TO TRANSFORM LIVES

MARY KATHERINE DOYLE, RSM

It Takes More than a Roof:
Mercy Housing's Mission to Transform Lives
Published by Mercy Housing
Denver, CO
MercyHousing.org

ISBN: 979-8-218-87654-8 (paperback)

SOCIAL SCIENCE / Activism & Social Justice

Edited by Elizabeth Allen.
Layout design by Asya Blue Design.
All copyright owned by Mercy Housing.

*For those who dream of a world where
everyone has a safe, affordable home—
and those who make it real, and to the residents
whose resilience, wisdom, and hope have shaped
every chapter of this story.*

CONTENTS

INTRODUCTION

Twenty months ago, I began a journey through forty years of history: The history of Mercy Housing, Inc. I wasn't sure what I would discover along the way or if the story would captivate the mind and challenge the spirit. Now twenty months later, I find that the journey has changed me, inspired me, and stirred in me a passion to be part of ending homelessness in my city, state, and nation. The stories and people I encountered on my journey have been courageous, committed, creative, and resilient.

No book can ever capture the scope of what is done daily through Mercy Housing. The work is so much more than building houses. It is a work that seeks to transform lives. When I began this project, I had no idea of the complexity involved in getting even one affordable housing property completed. I wondered why it seems to take so long. Now I know. From conception to completion can take anywhere from three to five years, but sometimes as long as ten years depending on how difficult it is to weave together financing, how demanding the regulatory policies are in any particular area, and how long it takes to build trust with the civic leaders, the neighborhood, and the future residents themselves.

Throughout the story I have tried to capture the essence of each stage: pre-development, development, and the transition to full residency. Each stage is unique. Only when such work is done in a collaborative style does a new property meet its promise. How Mercy Housing collaborates with others beyond the organization itself is another remarkable aspect of the story. Recognizing that no one organization has the capacity to end homelessness, Mercy Housing initiated a three-legged model: development, property management/resident services, and a Mercy loan component called Mercy Community Capital. The latter has loaned other non-profits monies to enable them to fund their own affordable housing properties or preserve apartment complexes that are at risk of being transformed into full rent properties.

Perhaps what impressed me most was the way in which the core values and mission of Mercy Housing are embedded in every aspect of the ministry. Respect, Justice, and Mercy guide every decision. Decisions are not made because they are expedient. They are made because they are right and needed. It is the dedication, commitment, and hard work of staff, donors, and partners that are the backbone of its success. Mercy Housing's Chief Executive Officer Ismael Guerrero puts it this way: "The sisters' vision, rooted in compassion, justice and service, continues to inspire and guide every step we take. We see the power of preserving our history while actively shaping the future, ensuring that the values of Mercy Housing remain strong."[1]

The story of Mercy Housing is best captured in the stories of lives touched and transformed. One story was particularly moving and illustrated for me why this ministry is so important. It is the story of Arnold Hampton, a Washington State Park Ranger for 25 years. Like many families, critical family illness changed his life. His wife, who was blind, was diagnosed with kidney failure and

Arnold decided to leave his career to care for her. Multiple trips for dialysis, the need for constant care, and all the demands of such an illness, rapidly depleted their savings. They downsized to a motor home but even that became unaffordable. Finally, they moved into their four-door sedan.

Arnold was lucky to have a circle of friends and co-workers to advocate for him. An article on homelessness, published by a local paper, highlighted his story. After its publication, his journey brought him to Lacey Community Action Network. A social worker referred Arnold and his wife to Mercy Housing Northwest. Arnold puts it simply: "I knew my wife's days were numbered. I didn't want her to die in that car. Our new home was a weight off our shoulders, and it meant my wife's final days could be spent in the dignity, love, and warmth of a home." Arnold's wife died a year later but not in the backseat of their car. She died surrounded by people she loved in a home of her own.[2]

The preservation of Mercy Housing's story takes a wide circle of collaborators. I am indebted to Jennifer Covert who has championed this undertaking since its inception; to Sister Patsy Harney RSM and Patricia O'Roark who interviewed so many of the early leaders of Mercy Housing and shared their own experience; the many current leaders of Mercy Housing who were gracious in sharing their wisdom about their work; to Jane Graf, the former CEO of Mercy Housing, who shared so much of her lived history of Mercy Housing; and Ismael Guerrero, current Chief Executive Officer of Mercy Housing, who has lent his support and wisdom to this process.

I am also immensely grateful to my faithful readers and responders who have made this a much better book: Sisters Marie Michele Donnelly RSM and Sister Anne Chester RSM, Patricia O'Roark, Jacquie Hoffman, Ismael Guerrero, Stefanie

Joy, Mark Angelini, Jane Graf, Parag Gupta, Patricia Cochran, Joe Rosenblum, Kate Peterson, Jeffrey Kohler, Anahi Gutierrez Chavez, and Jennifer Covert. Thanks also to my wonderful proofreader Elizabeth Allan, who provided a much-needed eye for mistakes!

It has been a privilege and blessing for me to be able to tell this story. I hope that you, the reader, will find it both informative and inspirational. Mercy Housing is a legacy ministry, carrying forward the work of its founding sisters. That mission now belongs to every staff member, board member, donor, and collaborator who create it anew every day. As you begin to explore this story yourselves, may you find the words of Ismael Guerrero resounding in your own spirit:

> We are carrying forward, paying forward, the rich heritage of service and compassion that the sisters invested in 40 years ago, and continue to invest in today. That commitment to service, and to excellence, is what being a legacy ministry means to me. It implies a deep commitment to the values and mission that have guided us from the beginning. At Mercy Housing, the sister's legacy is not a historical fact, it is a living, present and future reality that continues. It is about being a beacon of hope and continuing to make a positive impact on the lives of individuals and communities.[3]

CHAPTER 1

WE CAN DO BETTER...

Over 43,000 persons have safe, affordable housing today because one woman, Patricia O'Roark, was frustrated by the sea of human suffering she experienced as a Legal Aid Society lawyer. It was just at the beginning of the 1980s when a new type of homelessness was emerging.

Patricia, then Sister Timothy Marie, a Sister of Mercy, faced that reality every day in her office as desperate men and women sought help. In her own words:

> I was working at the Legal Aid Society in Omaha as a staff attorney and worked with families who had little to no help accessing affordable housing and were being evicted from where they were living at the time with little to no notice. The conditions they were living in were horrible. After talking with family after family and seeing how they were treated by some property management and owners, I thought, 'Lordy, I know we can do better than this.'[1]

Patricia O'Roark's urge to make a change in the lives of suffering people was fed and energized by the charism[2] she inherited from Catherine McAuley, foundress of the Sisters of Mercy. The Mercy charism found its expression in helping those most in need. Safe, secure housing was one of those pressing needs. To understand Patricia's urgent desire to provide for those who were unsheltered, one has to start with the woman who inspired her efforts, Catherine McAuley.

Catherine's efforts started even before she founded the Sisters of Mercy in 1831. Whether it was homeless orphans she found on the streets, like Ellen Corrigan and Ann Rice, or Mrs. Harper, a cranky and mentally unstable old woman, Catherine did what she could to provide them safe, stable housing. For Mrs. Harper and the two young orphans, that meant taking them into her own home at Coolock House located outside of Dublin's central district. Catherine's response to problems was practical, experiential, and spiritual. For her, housing and hospitality were linked.

Like Patricia O'Roark's frustration over her evicted clients, Catherine McAuley's commitment to the work of sheltering the vulnerable was fueled by the realities of her time. She didn't have a lot of patience with policies and practices that delayed help. To put it bluntly, she said: "The poor need help today, not next week."[3]

Catherine McAuley began her work just prior to Ireland's Great Potato Famine in 1845 but the problem of the unsheltered began long before that. Land was subdivided at the time of death, so farms began to shrink until they were no longer able to sustain families. Catholics, forbidden to own land by penal laws put in place during the Cromwellian era, could only rent their farms. When unable to pay their rents, Irish cottagers were evicted from their homes with nowhere else to go. Desperation led to almost half of the Irish population emigrating to other lands.

The pain and suffering of homelessness were not foreign to Catherine. She had a keen understanding of what the inner pain of losing your home was like, having experienced the emotional toll that housing insecurity inflicts upon the human spirit. Catherine's father was a successful contractor. The McAuley home was comfortable and secure but that was not to last. When she was just a young child, Catherine's father James McAuley died and upon his death, the surviving family embarked on a journey of downsizing. Elinor McAuley, Catherine's mother, did not possess adequate financial skills to manage the family monies, and family fortunes slowly eroded over time. She moved her family to smaller and smaller houses right up until the time of her own death.

England's economic policies, the emergence of *laissez-faire* dynamics, absentee landlords, lack of educational opportunities, and recurring potato blight drove rural populations in Ireland to financial ruin. Young unmarried women were particularly vulnerable when unable to access safe shelter. Left without monies, protector, or home, such young women became easy targets for exploitation. Catherine had first-hand knowledge of this reality.

As a young woman herself, Catherine found shelter as the house manager at Coolock House, the home of her employers, William and Margaret Callaghan. Once a young domestic servant came to Catherine desperately seeking safety from the unwanted sexual demands of the servant's employer. Try as she may, Catherine could not find safe shelter for the young girl that night. Whatever safe havens existed required that applicants be admitted only after the review of an admissions committee. In the words of Sister Mary Vincent Harnett, an early biographer of Catherine McAuley, the result was a "calamity."[4] She never saw the young girl again. The experience left Catherine with a strong resistance to rigid procedures as well as a passion to do what she could to provide for others in similar circumstances. It was at that point that Catherine determined, if she ever had the funds, she would build a small home for young domestic servants, providing not only shelter but safety.

Over one hundred years later, the crises faced by Patricia O'Roark's clients were rooted in similar realities. While Ireland of the 1830s had its famines and an uncontrolled economic policy of exporting essential foods, the United States in the late 1970s and early '80s suffered multiple recessions, seriously impacting the national economy. Governmental policy addressed the problem of the economy by making major cuts to the social network, especially in the area of housing and social services.

In the first half of the 1980s, multiple factors — including a lack of affordable housing, vanishing industries leading to loss of employment, high rents, the numbers of persons with mental health disabilities released into society from closing mental institutions, and a diminished social safety net — converged to create a new type of homelessness. The face of the unsheltered changed from single men in shabby hotels, "men of the road" or bag ladies, to younger persons, men, women, and children, who had homelessness foisted upon them. Many had been gainfully employed but rising costs, low wages, and personal tragedies were more than their resources could absorb. Homelessness was the monster at the door. No city was left untouched. In Denver, for example, evictions rose 800% in 1982 and "... hundreds of families lingered on waiting lists for public housing. Many were forced to live in shelters or the streets."[5] This type of trauma was not new. The vulnerability of Patricia O'Roark's clients in the 1980s mirrors that of Catherine McAuley's time.

For both Mercy women, homelessness was not just about the loss of physical shelter. It was also about what that state did to the human person and its contribution to the disintegration of the family. Jonathan Kozol alludes to such disintegration by sharing an interview with a homeless mother from Portland, Oregon, in his book, *Rachel and Her Children.* "We had good work until last year. Since then, we've had no home. Our kids were put in foster care."[6]

When her mother died, Catherine felt the sting of such dependency and powerlessness. Having no home of her own or monies to rent one, Catherine was dependent upon the generosity of family or friends to provide a roof over her head. She initially stayed with Owen Conway, her uncle, but found herself to be a burden upon his financially struggling family. Her uncle was faced with bankruptcy, and she was one more mouth to feed. Through this experience, she came to understand the anguish and insecurity of those who had to endure the powerlessness and insecurity of poverty.

Catherine's situation in some ways resembled that of today's hidden families who share a single apartment with multiple family members. They are often the invisible homeless, left without services and not counted in the numbers of unsheltered persons in a city or town. Fear creeps in, fear of saying the wrong thing, fear that children will misbehave and cause the host to send you away, fear that your presence will bring hardship to the legal resident. No day is free from anxiety. Catherine didn't need to worry about having children taken from her or being evicted from her new home, but she had to accept the religious hostility toward her faith held by the Armstrongs, her benefactors. Her brother and sister, also sheltered by the Armstrong family, solved the tension by converting to the faith of their hosts. For Catherine, that was not an option she would entertain.

Like the McAuley family, separated after the death of their mother, the homeless families of the 1980s lived with the constant fear that they would be separated. They not only had the normal fears around personal safety but sometimes feared that reaching out for help would result in further family disruption. Having your toddler sleeping on the streets with you was risky. Authorities saw it as putting your child in danger and you risked the little one being taken away by those same authorities. The only viable option for achieving a life that would thrive was finding safe, secure shelter.

Safe, secure housing was the vision of both Patricia O'Roark and Catherine McAuley but they shared a common dilemma. How do you find the resources to provide shelter to the persons right in front of you? In Catherine's case, it would come in a most unexpected way. Catherine had accepted an invitation from William and Margaret Callaghan to live with them as house manager and companion to Mrs. Callaghan. Catherine's employers did not share her Catholic faith, but both were people of faith. William, a Presbyterian, and Margaret, a Quaker, were rooted in the values of Christian charity. As such, the Callaghans were social-minded and supported Catherine's desire to bring food and education to the poor children in the area surrounding their home at Coolock. Over the years of her service with the family, Catherine became more than a manager and companion. She became like a daughter to the couple.

Catherine's desire to provide shelter for those in need grew during her time at Coolock House. Still raw from her inability to help the desperate servant who sought her help, she heard more stories of domestic servants seeking refuge from their desperate situations. Those stories urged her to do something concrete to address the need. Sister Mary Ann Doyle tells us that Mr.

Callaghan "had once spoken of leaving her a thousand pounds, and she thought, if she had that or even a few hundreds, she would hire a couple of rooms and work for and with her protegees."[7] For Catherine, it wasn't enough to provide a bed; one needed to provide skills with which the recipient could attain self-sufficiency. She saw too many young women obtain jobs only to lose them because they had not acquired the necessary training needed for the position. She wanted to change that scenario.

Catherine's initial hope of providing a few rooms to deserving domestic women grew beyond her imagining when, upon his death, William Callaghan left her his entire fortune, today worth an estimated value somewhere between two to four million dollars.[8] There was never a question in her mind about what she would do. She would build a home, a refuge for women in need of shelter, and provide a space where needy children could be taught the skills needed for them to avoid lives of dependency and poverty. Out of this deep desire, the House of Mercy on Baggot Street was born.

For the Sisters of Mercy who followed Catherine, her vision would point the way. She provided a model of shelter that would combine creating a home with supportive services to ensure that residents could move toward a secure future. It was not easy. Not everyone was excited about Catherine's project. No matter how lovely the House of Mercy might look, it brought a different social class to the wealthy part of Dublin. These new residents were poor, often uneducated, and didn't fit the mode of upscale society. The "not in my back yard" attitude was very much alive in the Dublin of her day. Even her brother James called the house she intended to build "Kitty's Folly."

If Catherine were a solo operator, the project most likely would have failed but she had a natural pattern of seeking collaborators in her works. A circle of women formed around her, many of whom would become the first Sisters of Mercy. She sought and received the support of many: Michael Blake, soon to be made Bishop of Dromore, Father Joseph Nugent, Frances Tighe, and Father Edward Armstrong, then priest-administrator of the parish.

With their support and advice, she leased for 150 years a plot of land on the corner of Baggot Street and Herbert Street. It would be close to the very people who would hire its residents as servants. The lease required a promise that the land would not be used for such things as "a Tavern, Ale-house, Soap-boiler, Chandler, Baker, Butcher, Distiller, Sugar Baker, Brewer, Druggist, Apothecary, Tanner, Skinner, Lime-Burner, Hatter, Silver-Smith, Copper Smith, Pewterer. Blacksmith or any other offensive or noisy Trade, Business or Profession whatsoever ..."[9] But a place to serve persons who were poor was not on the list!

Had the residents of her neighborhood known Catherine's intent, they most likely would have found ways in which to block the endeavor but Catherine kept secret her plans, even from her own family. She had a natural sense of how to approach things in a way that brought success to the enterprise. The architectural design of Baggot Street was part of that wisdom. So, what was the house like? On the outside it fit into the neighborhood with a stately exterior. It had three stories plus a basement. Dormitories were provided for women on the upper floor along with a second dormitory for children and eight small rooms for live-in volunteers assisting her in the ministry. Classrooms were found on the second floor. Those housed at Baggot Street, as well as children hidden and forgotten in the alleys and back streets of the area, were taught skills that would provide them with employment. The long tradition of supportive services found in

Mercy Housing Communities today can trace their origins back to this original model.

Unfortunately, even the large inheritance of Catherine wouldn't last forever. In fact, she used most of her monies within the first year of the ministry. At that point, she turned to philanthropy to close the gap. Fairs, charity sermons, and direct appeals were all part of the effort. All of this took place while controversy swirled around her. No one criticized the work; they only took exception to who was doing it. The problem: Catherine and her partners were living a pattern similar to that of the religious communities of the day, but they were not "nuns." In the opinion of her critics, that was unacceptable.

Catherine's passion for helping persons who were poor was infectious. Even before the House of Mercy opened, young women were drawn to join Catherine in the endeavor. Excited by the work and attracted to the type of lifestyle which was norm for Baggot Street residents, a circle of women emerged around Catherine. They weren't helpers; they were partners who Catherine trusted totally. Nothing more illustrates this vital partnership than Catherine's entrusting Mary Ann Doyle, her first partner in ministry, and Elizabeth Harley with the opening of the House of Mercy on September 24 1827 when, occupied by her own responsibilities as guardian for her nieces, nephews, and adopted children, she was unable to do so. Mercy's housing ministry was formally underway and so was the infant Order of Mercy.

There would be many challenges along the way. Some churchmen like Matthias Kelly, Father Armstrong's successor, strongly objected to her doing this ministry as a lay woman. Some saw her work as competing with the works of the Daughters of Charity. Money was always scarce, especially as client numbers swelled. Success generated more and more requests for services beyond

Dublin. Through it all, there existed a remarkable flexibility in Catherine, constantly adapting to the needs of the community served, a flexibility that led to her embracing life as a vowed woman religious within the Catholic church, as a Sister of Mercy, to ensure the continuity and future of the community.

As hard as initial undertakings can be, they provide a pattern for ongoing activity. Catherine's successes and challenges in meeting the needs of the unsheltered were replicated by the sisters who carried Mercy beyond Dublin. Sheltering those in need took a wide variety of forms: providing a home for orphans, housing domestic workers and women escaping from exploitation and prostitution, as well as the aged.

After the founding of the Order of Mercy in 1831, there was rapid expansion throughout Ireland. Among the foundations that replicated Catherine's House of Mercy were the Mercy Foundations in Cork, Limerick, and Kinsale. Each housing effort was unique to the need. In Limerick, a garrison town, a home for women who wanted to escape prostitution was vital; in Kinsale, an industrial school with boarders was most needed. Shelter, training, and assistance in finding employment were all part of the work.

From these Irish roots emerged a pattern which would characterize all later Mercy Housing endeavors. First, shelter would be provided; second, that shelter would be accompanied by education and training leading to self-esteem and self-sufficiency. For the unsheltered who had fallen into destructive patterns that robbed them of their dignity, an environment which fostered conversion of life was provided.

The story of these early Houses of Mercy reflects a belief that one must not stop at temporary solutions like providing a bed for the night but must wed that act of charity with a supportive and transformative combination of services that allow the recipients to change their situations. Providing shelter for those without a home became an integral part of tradition for Sisters of Mercy. One might say that it was Catherine McAuley's first ministry. It wasn't planned. It just happened as she encountered in the person before her the horrific suffering of the period. So it was for the sisters like Patricia O'Roark, who followed after Catherine.

This pattern of ministry started by Catherine was adapted to meet the unique needs of each location. The ministry of housing in the American mission was rooted in this vision. A cursory survey of Mercy ministries in the United States prior to 1920 reveals that, like its Irish prototype, the call to provide shelter to the unsheltered took a variety of forms: orphanages, homes for the aged, Houses of Mercy, Magdalen Asylums, and boarding opportunities for young girls from rural areas that sought education in Mercy academies. These ministries were not limited to just one area of the country but ranged from Buffalo, New York to St. Louis, Missouri; from San Francisco, California, to Washington D.C. and beyond to Portland, Oregon, and multiple places in between. One thing they all had in common. Like Catherine and like today's Mercy Housing, it was never about religious evangelizing or conversion. It was about service for anyone who was in need.

It was this heritage that shaped the vision of Patricia O'Roark. It gave her the courage and conviction that "We can do better." Not to attempt to do so would be unfaithful to the Mercy tradition. There were persons gravely in need, families on the verge of disintegration. There were seeds of despair and hopelessness being planted daily in the hearts and spirits of those who could not find shelter, let alone a place to call home. Patricia had no money. She had no benefactor that would leave her three million dollars. What she did have was a community of like-hearted sisters rooted in the same legacy. Now she just had to figure out what was the first step.

. . . .

For Your Reflection and Conversation

- As you reflect upon the story of Catherine McAuley, what aspects of her story do you see active in our own time?

- Patricia O'Roark was inspired to give her life and energies in service of those who are poor by the example of Catherine McAuley. Who has been your inspiration in pursuing the work you do in your life at this time? What is it that attracts you to his/her example?

CHAPTER 2

MOVING FROM FRUSTRATION TO ACTION

For some people, frustration leads to ulcers. That was not Patricia O'Roark's path. She made her frustration work for her, mobilized her energy, and decided to talk to someone who might have a path forward. That someone was Sister Norita Cooney, Provincial of the Mercy Province of Omaha. The timing was fortuitous. Change was moving across the Mercy Community in the U.S. as sisters tried to respond to the call of the Catholic Church to respond to the needs of the time. The expanding numbers of the unsheltered throughout the country was one of those critical needs.

At the time, the sisters were not the only ones looking at the needs of unsheltered persons. In 1975, the American Bishops published a statement called "The Right to a Decent Home: A Pastoral Response to the Crisis in Housing." The statement lifted up the urgency of the situation. Its opening words were:

> The United States is in the midst of a severe housing crisis. This is a broader, more pervasive, and more complicated phenomenon than the customary photographs of urban slums and rural shacks indicate.

It involves more people, more neighborhoods and communities than was thought to be the case even a few years ago. It touches millions of poor families who live in inhuman conditions, but it also involves many middle-income families whose ability to provide themselves with decent housing is being painfully tested.[1]

The document went on to raise startling statistics. These are just a few:

- One in every five families in the United States suffered from serious housing deprivation.

- Only 15% of American families could purchase a median-priced home.

- 4.7 million housing units lacked adequate plumbing facilities and 5 million families lived in overcrowded or shared housing.

- Two-thirds of substandard housing was in rural areas or in small towns. To be exact, 60% of all units without plumbing or experiencing overcrowding were found in these areas.

- An estimated 13.1 million American families suffered serious housing deprivation.

- In 1975, four out of five families with incomes below $5,000 suffered from some form of housing deprivation.[2]

Because of the critical need, the issue of persons' inability to obtain adequate housing gained urgency in the minds of Catholic church leaders, public advocates, and the Sisters of Mercy.

As providence would have it, a change in the circumstances provided an opportunity for the Sisters of Mercy to act upon the issue of homelessness. By the end of the 1970s across the United States, the number of young women seeking to become sisters had dropped significantly. The numbers of new members had been large when the sisters first built an administrative center called the Generalate of the Union of the Sisters of Mercy in Bethesda, Maryland, purchased in 1931. Having large numbers of new members entering was still true in the second half of the 1950s when the sisters sold the original building in order to provide a new administrative facility that was better suited to their needs. The facility had over 100 bedrooms for young sisters attending college in the Washington area during their training years. In the tradition of Catherine McAuley, a school for disadvantaged children was attached along with a chapel sufficient to seat 150 people, an archival repository, and other administrative areas needed for governance.[3]

Twenty years later, in 1977, it was time to reassess things. A feasibility study was conducted to determine the property's future direction. The study showed that the assessments supporting the operational costs of the building were now falling short, $273,618 short, to be exact.[4] It did not look as though the trend would reverse itself. The feasibility study also showed that the community was not unified around a course of action. Still, recommendations from the feasibility study needed to be presented to the 1979 Chapter.[5]

The study committee did its job and presented options for future usage within a context of enduring Mercy values. The committee, sharing its views in an article called "Committee Members Reflect Views: Generalate Building Symbol," reflected:

> We are challenged to develop a theology of 'letting go'
> so that as the poor reach out to take what they need
> we are not holding on to more than we need ... Are
> we willing to move into the future without this great
> center? Can our centering as Union be in the mission
> we share together rather than in the buildings we
> own together?[6]

Whatever decision would be made, it would be made on the basis of mission, not solely financial considerations. This was a value that would permeate all of Mercy's ministries. Mission always came first. In this instance, mission called for radical action. The unsheltered could not wait. Out of this urgency, Mercy Housing would shortly emerge.

Acting upon the recommendation of the study committee and with the encouragement of Sister Teresa Kane, the Union President, the decision was made to sell the property. It had not been an easy decision. Sister Catherine Kuper RSM. remembers it as one which was filled with emotion.[7] The site symbolized the identity of the Sisters of Mercy for many; for some a place of spiritual memory. She still remembers that delegates were asked to walk the property reflectively, holding the decision in prayer. When they returned to make the final decision, the vote was 63 to 5 in favor of selling the property. Sister Betty Barrett, chair of the feasibility committee, wrote to Sister Mary Jane Fisher:

> Never in my most hopeful moments did I think the
> decision to sell the land and buildings would be made
> so peacefully and almost totally by the Chapter body.
> I felt at the moment of the vote that we of the Union
> were facing a most significant event in our history.[8]

What fed the will to make such a change was the realization that monies from the sale of the property could make a difference for those in need. Priority was placed upon using the monies to address the issue of homelessness. As part of the decision, monies from the sale were to be allotted to each of the provinces. Each of the nine provinces of the Union was free to use the money according to the needs of their own area. The "how" was left up to each of the individual provinces of the Union.

The responses arising in provincial communities were diverse but housing was a high priority. Providing shelter for those in need was not a new ministry for the sisters. Even in 1947, a report to the Chapter indicated that the sisters of the Union conducted thirteen homes for the elderly, serving 788 men and women.[9] Five years later, the Baltimore providence would add Stella Maris Hospice to that number. The Hospice added assisted living and independent living apartments for elderly people to Mercy's housing efforts. Now it was time for the Province of Omaha to decide what path to take in addressing homelessness. That path would be to provide affordable housing for the vulnerable.

Sister Norita urged Patricia to submit a proposal to the Omaha Provincial Chapter of 1980. She told Patricia: "Don't think of this as an individual sister's ministry. Think bigger. Think about it as a community-sponsored ministry."[10] Patricia, taking Sister Norita's advice to heart, began to prepare a proposal that could be submitted to the approaching chapter. She remembers being nervous about her presentation. As she puts it: "We were committing to an idea with few particulars attached."[11] There was no map for what she was asking. In fact, she notes that "housing development was not even in their vocabulary."[12] Drawing on the urgency of the Bishop's statement on "The Right to a Decent

Home" and her own experience, she crafted the proposal. It read:

> Because the providing of adequate housing is a major social need at the present time, and
>
> Because "sheltering the homeless" is consistent with the tradition established by Catherine McAuley, with the service goals of the Omaha Province, and with the urgent call from the institutional church to respond to the needs of the materially poor,
>
> THE OMAHA PROVINCE CHAPTER OF 1980, IN RESPONSE TO THE CRY OF THE POOR ENDORSES THE MINISTRY OF HOUSING AS ANOTHER OF OUR CORPORATE INSTITUTIONAL MINISTRIES,

In order to establish this service among our other present services, this Chapter:

1. DIRECTS THE PROVINCIAL ADMINISTRATION TEAM TO ESTABLISH A TASK FORCE:
   a. to define the goals, scope and direction of this ministry;
   b. to establish criteria for the sponsorship of this ministry which would be consistent with the goals of the Institute and province as well as with the call to justice;
   c. to report regularly to the Provincial Administrative Team and periodically to the Chapter Delegates for assessment and evaluation.

2. DIRECTS THE PROVINCIAL ADMINISTRATIVE TEAM TO RECRUIT A COMMUNITY MEMBER to act as staff to the task force in the work of gathering data, researching existing resources and projects, and initiating programs in this area.[13]

The proposal was one of two under consideration by the Chapter body.

Sister Catherine Kuper remembers that the first proposal dealt with when novices might have voting privileges at Chapter. That discussion went back and forth for over an hour and a half before it was voted upon. The housing proposal was next. It was Sunday morning when Patricia, then Sister Timothy Marie, approached the body with the proposal and its accompanying rationale. The decision took 20 minutes![14]

What was notable was that there was little to no discussion. Usually, such matters stirred up lots of questions, concerns, and hesitancies. That was not the case. In less than 30 minutes, the sisters embraced a ministry which would grow far beyond their imagining at the time. Patricia notes: "When we passed this, we really didn't know what it would involve. It was a dream."[15]

When asked how such a major decision could be made so smoothly, Sister Rita Parks, then part of the leadership team for the Province, immediately attributed the action to two factors: the credibility of Patricia O'Roark, which arose from her lived experience, and the desire of the sisters to take a corporate stand on something, to speak with a common voice.[16] Sister Catherine Kuper adds to that perception, saying: "Patricia's ability to capture a need was critical. There was a radical and pragmatic ascent to answering the needs of the time."

The initial moment of Mercy Housing's founding provided a lens through which it would grow. Whatever was done was in response to need. It would grow organically. It would also be rooted in the tradition of Catherine McAuley, her values of respect, compassion, and justice, as well as being grounded in the social teachings of the Catholic Church which affirms that every person is entitled to live a life of dignity, a life that affirms his or her worth as a human person. What the founding moment did not determine was the "how" of the task. That would be left to the implementation of the Provincial Leadership Team.

When the Provincial Leadership Team met after the Chapter, they were faced with the challenge of how to put flesh on the housing proposal just adopted. Sister Norita Cooney explained:

> After we passed the proposal at the chapter to look at housing as another corporate ministry of the Sisters of Mercy, we also decided at that time that we would set aside half a million dollars to get this venture off the ground. Now, the reason for the half a million was because we really wanted it to be successful and when you are in the housing ministry, you can't go far with $10,000 or $20,000 or even $100,000 dollars. So, our intent was really to do everything that we could to try and make an impact on the housing needs of the people in the communities that we serve. And we felt that we had to set aside significant dollars to do that. And for us, that was significant dollars.[17]

Having designated the funding, the team now had to decide how to use it. One idea was to use the monies to support the efforts of organizations already engaged in affordable housing. Another was for the sisters to become engaged in the affordable housing field themselves. There was no clear path. What was needed was an experienced leader for the effort.

While Patricia O'Roark might have been an obvious possibility, she was not available due to her responsibility as Director of the Legal Aid Society of Northeast Nebraska. The leadership team, committed to the success of the ministry, elected to invite one of their top hospital administrators to leave her ministry and walk into this unknown sphere. Her name was Sister Mary Terese Tracy. Sister Terese describes the invitation this way:

> Shortly after the proposal to establish housing as a sponsored ministry was approved by [our community] in the fall of 1980, I received a phone call ... asking whether I would consider helping to put together a plan of action to implement that decision ... My assignment was to facilitate the development of a plan to address the housing needs of the poor.[18]

Sister Mary Terese was considered the ideal leader to establish Mercy Housing. She had vast experience in healthcare and was on the board of directors of multiple Catholic healthcare systems in the country, as well as on the board of Catholic Health Initiative. In addition, she served as head administrator of the Mercy Medical Center in Nampa, Idaho. In this capacity, she was in touch with hospitals throughout the United States.[19] Her move from healthcare administration to affordable housing would set a pattern for many of the Sisters of Mercy who became involved with Mercy Housing in the years to come.[20] Leaving a cherished and successful ministry and leaping into the unknown would become a familiar choice of Mercy Housing's pioneer sisters.

In selecting Sister Mary Terese to lead the fledgling organization, the Leadership Team had more than transferable skills in mind. Sister Catherine Kuper shares that "they were looking for someone to get something done and knew that she could get something done!"[21] She went on to say: "Terese was open, friendly and firm in vision. She was all about empowering people. She stood tall and straight, and when she spoke you listened."[22] Sister Jeanne Ward notes that: "Terese looked stern, even intimidating but she was not what she looked like. She passed on the love of the housing ministry, the passion for it."[23] Sister Rita Parks sums up what calling Sister Terese meant, saying: "She was one of our strongest and most forward thinking. It took such courage to give up such a rewarding ministry as hospital administration to take on something no one, including herself, knew anything about."[24] The choice was a stroke of genius as well as a commitment to Mercy Housing's future. In looking back upon that decision, Sister Norita Cooney reflects:

> There wasn't any hesitancy on her part ... she knew she was good at what she did, but she didn't mourn moving from healthcare. She said, 'I'd be willing to take that on.' And she was very excited about it. And I think we were just so blessed, so blessed to have her assume that responsibility. And I really think that's what made all the difference ... in the direction of Mercy housing and how it all developed into the future.[25]

Sister Mary Terese's task was threefold. She had to first create a plan that others could buy into. She had to assemble a team with the foresight, skills, and passion needed to make the new ministry a reality. Lastly, she had to implement the plan. The manner in which she did this is captured in a series of memos she wrote during the beginning days of her administration. The first memo written on October 2, 1981, was tinged with humor as she told the sisters that while no building was under construction, "We have begun to construct an excellent plan!"[26] That plan was not the sole creation of Sister Terese. She worked together with a Task Force of housing professionals, neighborhood organizers, attorneys, and interested province members. Among that small group were folks who would play a significant role in the ministry going forward: Sisters Patricia O'Roark, Stella Neill, Joan Martin, Jeanne Ward, Jean Beste, BVM, and Jim Tomlinson.[27] In just a short period, they shaped the mission and goals of the ministry. Sister Terese then shared with the community the mission and goals, which had been approved by the Provincial Administration.

They were simple and clear:

MISSION—

The Sisters of Mercy, Province of Omaha, are committed to provide leadership and be directly involved in serving the emotional, physical, social, and spiritual needs of the poor through the RSM Housing Ministry.

GOALS—

1. To create and maintain an ongoing organizational support system to ensure continuity of the RSM Housing Ministry to the poor.

2. To provide RSM personnel committed to leadership and direct service to the poor through the RSM Housing Ministry

3. To provide holistic programs and services to meet the human needs of the poor and empower them to assume responsibility for and control of their own environment.[28]

It was a tall order to fulfill.

The second ministry update began to paint for the community a picture of the realities which had to be faced. In her second update to the community, Sister Mary Terese named a particularly troubling dynamic: "Because of recent changes in regulations, present owners of federally funded housing can now convert buildings to more profitable ventures. This results in the poor being evicted from housing which was originally intended to meet their needs."[29]

The facts were staggering. "In New York City, with a total of nearly two million rental units, there were half a million legal actions for eviction during 1983. Half of these actions were against people on welfare, four-fifths of whom were paying rents above the maximum allowed by welfare."[30] To make matters worse, federal funds for building or rehabilitating low-income housing and support of low-income housing dropped from $32 billion to $7 billion between 1980 and 1987 in the beginning years of Mercy Housing.[31]

At the time, eviction laws tended to favor the landlord, not the resident. While these laws were causing suffering, there was another housing situation that positively infuriated Patricia O'Roark and which contributed to her passion to do something about housing. Government contracts were awarded to landlords to provide affordable housing for persons in need. Commonly known as the Section 8 program, the federal government subsidized the difference between the monthly rent a low-income family could afford to pay (roughly, 25% of monthly income) and the prevailing market rate. Federal oversight of the landlord's responsibility was often lax, and unscrupulous landlords simply pocketed the monies without providing adequate services to the tenants. Such landlords ignored broken plumbing, peeling paint, and unhealthy conditions in their buildings.

Tenants frequently didn't know or understand their rights. In one case, sisters teaching in a summer religious education program noticed that children in one family frequently came to class dirty, disheveled, and smelly. When they went to visit the family in their rental dwelling, they discovered that the landlord had disconnected the water, and the family had to walk one mile to a gas station to get clean water. Since the sisters themselves had paid the water and rental bill, the landlord was forced to meet his obligations. These situations were frustrating to social service workers, dispiriting to tenants, and blatantly illegal. As Patricia puts it, "The helpers weren't helping."

Given the dual reality of diminishing affordable housing units and the sometimes-squalid conditions of subsidized housing, Sister Terese shared with the community and its partners that, "Our response will be to acquire management control of these properties in order to preserve them for the poor ... and ensure that social justice values prevail."[32] The memo went on to say that the ventures which would be pursued required that the Mercy Management practices needed to be firmed up and Sisters of Mercy needed to be recruited as managers.

First, Sister Terese looked for two or three sisters who were willing to learn "creative ways of serving in neighborhood or rural areas."[33] The role of these sisters would be to become a resource for others who wished to organize activities which would bring pressure to bear on individuals or institutions engaging in unjust practices.[34] Another four sisters were to be recruited to develop expertise in housing management. Once trained, they would develop mercy training sites as well as Mercy Management, Consultation and Services. Every sister recruited was asked to commit to three to five years of service on a full-time basis. The recruitment process wasn't complicated. Sr. Terese sent out a flyer in the province mailings that said if you are interested in housing management, housing development, or neighborhood organizing, let us know.

The invitation which went out in January 1982 once more reflected the humor of Sister Terese. It was headed: WANTED … ALIVE.

By the end of 1981, Sister Terese had made significant progress in establishing the structure needed to sustain the ministry. The mission was defined, goals established, recruitment for sister managers begun, and, in December 1981, Mercy Housing was incorporated. In addition to these structural pieces needed to firmly establish the new ministry, interest from the monies for housing was allotted for a grant process specially designated for projects that had no other source of funding. These grants were rooted in the same values which grounded the Mercy Housing Ministry as a whole: community engagement, participation of the beneficiaries, and a priority on serving those who were poor.

Now what remained was full implementation of the vision and plan. To do that required making the map by walking. The community eagerly waited to see where that road would lead.

. . . .

For Your Reflection and Conversation

- Patricia O'Roark's passionate response to need moved from an unshaped idea to a community commitment. Based on your reading, what factors made such a movement possible? Are these factors still significant today?

- Patricia drew upon key sources like "The Right to a Decent Home" to support her proposal to her sisters. In proposing a new initiative or service line to Mercy Housing Board members, what documents or sources would you use to develop the proposal today?

CHAPTER 3

IT TAKES MORE THAN A ROOF...

How does a house become a home? As the Sisters of Mercy began their housing ministry, that was a key question before them. It wasn't enough just to provide a roof, four walls, a bathroom, and a locked door. It had to provide more: a restored sense of connection, help to reengage with society, a place to feel secure, safe, and valued. First, though, basic safe shelter had to be provided. With a vision defined, the work began.

Boise, Idaho might seem like an unlikely spot to start a new housing ministry, but it was well suited to that intent. Not only was there need, but there were also networks and mentors that could lend support for the sisters' first ventures into the world of real estate. No one was a more significant partner than James Tomlinson. Tomlinson, a real estate professional in Idaho, was well known to Sister Terese and possessed the experience in affordable housing development and property management that all the Mercy pioneers lacked. It was his sage advice that guided the way.

It would have been easy to focus the ministry on use of the initial $500,000 to fund the work of other agencies and groups working on affordable housing. It would have been simpler, too. Jim thought otherwise and thought more expansively. "Don't give the money away. I'll show you how to do this."[1] And showing how he did! He helped the sisters learn how to manage properties themselves as well as how to leverage their money and develop on a large scale. He strongly believed that it was important for them to own properties, not just manage them. His wisdom, experience, and friendship led the sisters to invite him to be a member of the ministry's first board of directors. It also set in motion a pattern of collaborative partnering that would characterize Mercy Housing going forward.

In December 1981, Sister Terese took a major step forward by purchasing Mercy Housing's first affordable family housing properties, Wylie Street Station and Treehouse, both located in Boise, Idaho. Together the properties comprised 65 units. The purchase of the properties was possible through what is called a syndication process. Simply defined, real estate syndication occurs when a group of investors pools together their capital to jointly purchase a large real estate property. Apartments, mobile home parks, land, self-storage units, and other real estate assets are some of the investment opportunities available through syndications. In the case of the Wylie Street Station and Treehouse properties, the infant Mercy Housing, Inc., after being officially incorporated in December 1981, partnered with DBSI, a Meridian property management and investment company.

With property in hand, the work began in earnest. Tomlinson and Associates helped the sisters learn the ins and outs of property management and actually managed the property for Mercy Housing in the initial months prior to management by the sisters taking root. As Jim Tomlinson describes it: "The company shepherded them as the sisters all tried to get on top of things."[2]

Tomlinson explains that it wasn't all work. He fondly remembers fun times like fishing trips with the sisters at a nearby reservoir.

Three other communities quickly joined the Wylie Street and Treehouse properties: Pioneer Square in Boise, Idaho (44 units); Shadow Mountain in Idaho City (14 units); and Grand Cascade in American Falls (64 units). These holdings were spread out, and their prior owners sometimes had a very different sense of property management than the new Mercy Housing had. In the field of affordable housing, some owners, looking for profits, were concerned about investment return and not service. Tomlinson explains that there was a fragmented group of developers who were building houses and apartments but not caring for them well.

Mercy Housing brought a different vision. It was a ministry committed to fostering communities of dignity, safety, and growth. Initially, this was the task of sisters who volunteered to work in property management. Their responsibilities were myriad. Sister Terese outlined what they might be doing in an invitatory memo written in January 1981, as she sought out seven sisters to give three to four years to the new endeavor. She wrote:

FOUR SISTERS WILLING TO COMMIT 3-5 YEARS
TO THE MERCY HOUSING MINISTRY WITHIN
THE PROVINCE BOUNDARIES

... Interested in learning creative ways of managing housing developments to insure the provision of housing for the poor while, at the same time, offering holistic educational, health, and other support programs needed by the poor to enable and empower them to control their own environment and make the major decisions affecting their lives, thus enhancing their dignity as persons and promoting their independence.

This type of involvement will require management expertise such as, but not limited to, the following: Placing of Residents; Leasing, Rentals; Enforcement of Lease Agreements, Rules, and Regulations; Maintain Highest Occupancy Rates Possible at All Times; Handle Evictions When Necessary; Maintenance to Insure Residents' Satisfaction (Grounds and Buildings); Assume Responsibility for Residents' Problems/Complaints Inspect Apartments; Quarterly Review Waiting List of Applicants; Regularly Insure Good Channels of Communication Between Manager and Residents; Oversee All Services and Programs; Comply with Government Standards, Regulations and Reporting Meet All Health, Safety and Fire Regulations; Supervise Controller to Provide Workable System to Process Billings, Payments, Payroll, Rent Management, Reports and Budget; Supervise Staff; Conduct Weekly Staff Meetings; Plan In-service Programs; Resolve Conflicts; Hire/ Terminate employees; Annual Evaluations and Wage and Benefit Programs; Negotiate Contracts; Purchase Equipment and Supplies; Assume Fund-Raising Responsibilities; Participate in Professional Meetings, Board Meetings, Etc.; Participate in Province Mercy Housing Ministry Activities; Participate in National, State, Civic and Church Activities Which Will Foster the Improvement of Housing for the Poor.[3]

And this was just for the property management side of the ministry. Sister Terese had developed a different list of skill sets for those sisters who wished to work more closely with development processes and supportive services. Here she both defined the job and listed the skills needed:

THREE SISTERS WILLING TO COMMIT 3-5 YEARS TO THE MERCY HOUSING MINISTRY WITHIN THE PROVINCE BOUNDARIES

… Interested in learning creative ways of serving in neighborhood or rural areas and to be trained in skills which will empower poor people to protect their rights and their neighborhoods or rural areas.

… how to help eradicate discriminatory practices and provide holistic educational, health, and other support programs needed by the poor to assist them in achieving human dignity.

… how to involve the poor in a participative style that will empower them to control their own environment and make major decisions affecting their lives.

… how to assist the poor to gain a greater measure of independence and justice.

This type of involvement will require training or expertise in skills such as, but not limited to, the following: Basic Philosophy of Organizing Issue Development; Leadership Development; The Art of Negotiation; Developing Winning Strategies; Coalition Building; Organization on Reinvestment; Fund Raising; Organizing on Insurance; Redlining;

> Initiating and Maintaining a Community Development Corporation; Housing Development and Rehabilitation; Organizing Credit Unions; Organizing Cooperatives; Programming - Holistic Concepts; Participation in Province Mercy Housing Ministry Activities; Participation in National, State, Civic and Church Activities Which Will Foster the Improvement of Housing for the Poor Influencing Legislation.[4]

The daunting lists would make anyone think twice before jumping into the new ministry, but by February, Sister Terese had her seven volunteers: Sisters Joan Martin, Jeanne Christensen, Regis Leahy, Joan Marie Martin, Jeanne Ward, Marilyn Ross, and Mary Drey. Drawn from healthcare, education, and social service ministries, none were really experienced in housing development or property management. It was "learn as you go."

To support and prepare her intrepid pioneers, Sister Terese worked on finding internships which would provide them with essential knowledge and experience. Potential internship sites were located all over the country, ranging from Denver, Colorado, to Visalia, California; from Yuma, Arizona, to Yakima, Washington; and from Philadelphia, Pennsylvania, to Chicago, Illinois.

The internships covered a variety of housing situations. An internship possibility in Hancock, Maine, H.O.M.E, focused on helping people with employment and the development of collective industries. Warren Village in Denver focused on single parents while the Pacific Institute for Community Organizations offered participants skills in the art of grass roots organizing. The Midwest Academy offered folks a five-day workshop called "Organizing for Social Change." There were endless possibilities from which to choose. Each sister was encouraged to select the internship/s that best suited both her needs and skills.

The job requirements list shared by Sister Terese painted more than a picture of what the ministry would be like. In the lists were embedded values and practices, values like empowerment, human dignity, mutual participation, and justice, which would shape the ministry going forward. Property managers were to be more than caretakers of buildings. They were responsible for fostering the growth and development of vital communities. Supportive programs were highlighted as a core element. The support was to enable and empower the residents to control their own environment, as well as to provide skills in decision-making so that they could take control of their lives.

Developers were charged with serving populations and neighborhoods in such a way that they would be empowered to protect their rights as well as their neighborhoods. Everything was to be done in a participative, collaborative, and empowering style. These were wonderful words on paper, but it was up to the first seven pioneer sisters and their partners to translate them into day-to-day practice.

Sisters Joan Martin, Jeanne Ward, and Mary Drey were among the first to plunge in. Joan Martin was Mercy Housing's second employee. Initially she interned at Wylie Street Station in Boise to learn about property management. An investment company then managed Wylie Street Station. Sister Joan remembers one of her first experiences was receiving a memo from the company that "lawns had to look good."[5] In her opinion, the company was more concerned about investor interests and looking good than providing services to the residents. Sister Jeanne Ward, who worked with Sister Joan in Boise, would go a step further in saying that some property management companies only cared about "curb appeal."[6] While placing high value on external appearances, they cared little about the state of the inside residences.[7] As soon as Mercy Housing purchased the properties, Sister Joanne cancelled the contract with that company and, with the support of Jim Tomlinson's company, began to shape the future Mercy Property Management component of the ministry.

The internships were about learning what worked and what didn't work. While Sister Joan was beginning her work in Boise, Sister Jeanne was engaged in a property management internship at Warren Village in Denver. It was a single-parent high-rise for women and children. At Warren Village, operated by a faith community, Sister Jeanne did not have to fight to have the welfare of her residents be given high priority, but she did have to work to create an understanding among the residents themselves that they shared responsibility for making the community what they desired. Sister Jeanne's internship provided moments of shock as well as moments of satisfaction. One particular episode was etched in her memory forever. She vividly recalls the day when a little girl, a twin, fell out of a third story window and was badly injured. The little one, perched on top of her bunk bed, had managed to push a screw out of the window screen and fell from the unprotected window. Sister Jeanne reflects: "I grew up that day. On the way home from visiting her in the hospital, I pulled over and just sobbed."[8]

One positive thing did emerge from the accident. It taught all the residents the importance of both taking care of their residence and watching out for each other. That learning was reinforced when a mother was found banging her daughter's head against the wall of an elevator. It was evident that residents needed to be there for each other. Little by little, a community of support and caring began to be built. It was rewarding to see residents come together to make sure that mothers knew they could get help from other residents when they reached a breaking point. Gradually the mothers supported each other by offering babysitting, small acts of support, and kindness.

For nine months, from August 1982 until April of the following year, Warren Village was a training ground for Sister Jeanne. She was exposed to property management's nitty-gritty, day-to-day challenges. By February 1983, Mercy Housing had established Mercy Services Corporation as a separate entity to deal with property management. In time, Sister Joan, Mercy Services Corporation's newly appointed director, came from Boise to support Sister Jeanne's efforts to establish solid family services. Today Mercy Housing calls such services "resident services." Sister Jeanne recalls that one of the problems involved residents having male visitors staying overnight in their apartments, a practice that was forbidden. When Sister Joan impressed upon the residents that violating that rule would lead to eviction, one resident quickly responded: "But what are we going to do about our hormones!"[9] Sister's response was that they would have to find another way to address that!

One of the insights Sister Jeanne learned at Warren Village was the essential role that community building played in the success or failure of a housing complex. In her opinion, it was essential. She had seen the result of property management that failed to have the residents as the focus and lacked effective Resident Councils. In Omaha, such a situation resulted in the condemnation of the building, leaving residents with only three days to find new housing before the building was boarded up. Sister Jeanne says that hundreds of people were impacted, but that was not important to slum landlords for whom it was all about the money.[10]

Mercy Housing provided an alternative way of addressing housing needs. The first sister property managers experimented with approaches, programs, and policies that could bring residents into a community that was safe, secure, and empowering. As Resident Councils identified needs or desires, Mercy Housing's property managers could assist them in acquiring the skills to bring those to fruition. Managers and residents joined together in addressing the needs and hopes of the community.

The internship at Warren Village came to an early conclusion in April 1983, when Sister Jeanne was needed to help Sister Joan in Boise. With properties now numbering five separate housing communities, there was too much work to do for one person. Sr Jeanne's first week was marked by a major problem. She was faced with a geyser gushing in the parking area of Grand Cascade. Sister Joan had just left the day before for a short break and, newly arrived, Sister Jeanne didn't have a network of contacts in the new site. Jim Tomlinson came to the rescue and found someone to fix the broken pipe.

This wasn't her first encounter with unexpected situations. One day she arrived at Pioneer Square to find a two-year-old child on top of the roof watching traffic go by. The toddler had gained access to the roof because her family residence lacked a screen on the window. One of the lasting lessons from such events was that properties needed to be kept in excellent condition if you wanted residents to take care of them. Missing screens, broken fixtures, or peeling paint not only created potential safety hazards for the residents but also didn't motivate the community to keep their apartments safe and secure.

Shortly after Sister Joan went to minister in Boise, Sister Mary Drey, just a novice[11] at the time, along with Sister Marilyn Ross, her novice minister, accepted internships with the Blue Hill Housing Corporation in Kansas City, Missouri. Sister Marilyn was interested in the development side of the ministry while

Sister Mary wanted to focus on resident services. As Mary Drey describes it: "It was a time of exploration. We were trying to figure out what Mercy Housing would be like. We were sent to see what was happening in the field. Sister Terese encouraged us and we shared our learnings with her as we went along."[12]

Sisters Marilyn and Mary began their work under the supervision of Sister Jean Beste BVM, who had also been part of the initial task force. Blue Hills was a complex of rehabbed duplexes. While the renovated duplexes looked fine, the neighborhood left much to be desired. Sister Mary remembers the neighborhood as having a problem with gangs and trash. The area was in bad shape, and it was her job to assist in creating an environment in which the residents could come together to build a better neighborhood. The progress was slow and somewhat discouraging.

After a few months, Bishop Sullivan approached Sister Mary to take on a different position, this time in Wayne Miner, the worst public housing complex in Kansas City at the time. Here she could explore how community development might play an important part in Mercy Housing going forward. Bishop John Sullivan provided a $10,000 grant toward the development of better resident services at the facility. Betty Scott, President of the Tenant Association, and Mary were to work together to see what could be done.

It was a formidable task. Wayne Miner was a major challenge. Less than 30 years after it was built, it was in deplorable condition and authorities considered abandoning it as affordable housing and using it for a prison.

> Completed in 1960, Wayne Miner was built to house 738 families in its towers and 74 town houses. But, as one official put it, 'It was never more than 60 percent occupied because it developed a bad reputation early.'[13]

While the property was meant to bring about urban-renewal, Jed Stander, then executive director of the local housing authority lamented: ''What occurred was that it created blight in a different form.[14]

It was here at the troubled housing complex that Mary Drey, working side by side with Betty Scott, learned the challenges and realities of working within public institutions. Among the opportunities emerging from their joint efforts were a soup kitchen, community garden, revolving fund for rental assistance, and an on-site college and GED program for mothers and daughters to attend together. In spite of such undertakings, however, Mary's learnings confirmed Tomlinson's insight that if Mercy Housing was to achieve its goals, the sisters needed to own the properties. To fulfill the hopes and visions which prompted the founding of Mercy Housing, the freedom to shape both development and management policies and practices was critical.

Not all the pioneers had experiences comparable to that of Wayne Miner. During that same time period, Sister Jeanne Christenson was focusing on scattered-site housing, a type of housing where each dwelling was separate and scattered throughout an area not concentrated in one neighborhood. Sister Jeanne, trained in social work, had been working with Ecumenical Housing Production Corporation (EPIC), a faith-based organization that provided affordable rental housing. At first, she interned but soon became part of the staff. Here she learned the ins and outs of the affordable housing field. What EPIC did was to purchase abandoned or badly damaged single-family homes, rehab them, and rent them to families through the Department of Housing and Urban Development (HUD)'s Section 8 program. The homes were purchased most often through courthouse auctions, bank foreclosures, or land trust properties. It was this model that Sister Jeanne contributed to the early efforts of Mercy Housing.

With Sister Jeanne as its champion, the Kansas City outreach was the first Mercy Housing undertaking beyond Idaho. Vastly different from the high-rise Wayne Miner housing, it followed the model of EPIC. The work paralleled that of Habitat for Humanity. Sister Jeanne explains: "Habitat did the same type of work but for purchase. We provided another path through rentals."[15] Collaboration with Habitat for Humanity fostered a sense of pride in both home and neighborhood. Sister Jeanne put it this way: "You wanted kids coming home from school proud to say: 'That's where I live!'"

Like most early beginnings, Sister Jeanne had a bare minimum of resources with which to work. Risen Christ parish offered her an empty parish office and, with a typewriter and her phone in hand, Sister Jeanne began to establish connections in the neighborhood. Other parishes supplied a core of volunteers to help with the renovation of properties. Sister Terese Tracy believed in and supported Sister Jeanne's efforts with a Mercy Housing Inc. $35,000 line of credit. This line of credit eventually resulted in 92 units of safe, affordable family rental housing in metro Kansas City, Missouri. Along the way, Sister Jeanne had to obtain a real estate license in order to make this happen.

Significant differences in the model developed by Sister Jeanne Christenson and the model that would be normative for Mercy Housing in the future emerged from the focus on resident services. Sister Jeanne Ward explained that Mercy Housing had adopted a model of pastoral property management which was more effective and successful when the community was centralized in one building or housing proximity. It was easier to gather the community together and provide centralized programming. The scattered-site housing model also had a pastoral element to it but was more individualized. Sister Jeanne Christensen explains: "Once I visited a home and found the baby confined to her crib. When I asked why, the mother explained that she had no diapers and didn't want the baby to wet the floor."[16] Providing diapers was an easy fix. Sister went on to say: "You did what you could to help."

Working with 92 homes and their residents was never easy but, for the most part, Sister Jeanne found them great to work with. There were failures here and there. Once, she was contacted by the gas company and asked to help a young mother and baby find shelter. After going through all the steps necessary, the mom was settled into a recently renovated house. Shortly afterward, complaints began to come in about the house and possible drug use. Bringing members of a drug task force with them, both Sister Jeanne and Sister Joan Marie Martin went to check on the situation. Not only did they find drugs being sold, but a prostitution ring had set up business there as well. Eviction was immediate.[17]

Like her peer sister pioneers, Sister Jeanne Christensen picked up vital learnings from her ministry. One was the absolute necessity of collaboration and networking. To do the work meant you had to be connected to the folks who would provide what was needed. You not only had to learn to network but you had to learn to negotiate. Since most projects required doing much with little, you always had to look for the best deal you could find. Sometimes, Sister Jeanne notes, you had to walk away.

After nine years, Sister Jeanne left the housing ministry, but not without taking lasting memories. When asked what strikes her most from these early years, Sister Jeanne was quick to respond: "Sister Terese Tracy! Without her, there would be no

Mercy Housing."[18] Thinking back, she shared what still inspires her: "The courage of the troop of us that said: 'Why not? Let's see what we can do.'"[19] She continues: "We had to read the signs of the time and really understand how things work. To be honest, we didn't know what we were stepping into. We just knew we needed to do it. You can't be faint of heart and you can't be naïve."[20]

Completing the pioneer circle of Mercy Housing's early sisters are Sisters Joan Marie Martin and Mary Regis Leahy. Coming from an education background, Sister Joan Marie began her time in housing by interning at Northeast Kansas Community Action Program in Horton, Kansas, and then at Southwest Iowa Regional Housing Authority in Creston, Iowa. These rural internships prepared her to take on responsibility for a new project in Alamosa, CO. It was similar to the projects shepherded by Sister Jeanne Christensen in Kansas City. Preparing the homes was made possible through a $15,000 block grant and sweat equity from the soon-to-be residents. All the early Mercy pioneers had to become adept at such things as painting, plumbing, dry-walling, and anything else that came up.

Sister Joan Marie did not stay in Alamosa long. By October 1983, she was sent to Twin Falls, Idaho, to manage 105 scattered-site houses. Like her peers, Sister quickly saw that you have to plant a sense of pride in residents if you are to succeed or risk the frustration of property damage and neglect. Again, with the homes scattered over a wide region, it was challenging to keep on top of all the various resident needs and situations.

When asked about the hardest part of her ministry, Sister Joan Marie was quick to reply: "Evictions."[21] What was especially difficult were situations in which parents lost custody of their children. Walking the line between enforcing regulations and working to give folks a chance to change was hard. One significant learning garnered from Sister Joan Marie's experience was that you could not successfully combine the role of property manager with that of a social worker. In the initial days of the ministry, that happened, but lived experience showed that separating those roles was more beneficial.

Sister Mary Regis Leahy was the last of the original circle to begin her work at Mercy Housing, starting her internship in August 1984. Coming from parish religious education, she wanted to serve in a different capacity. Sister Terese welcomed this seventh volunteer and, after Sister Mary Regis's completion of a Real Estate Course, assigned her to intern with Brothers Redevelopment in Denver. Sister Mary Regis shared that the brothers were very much into paint-a-thon which they had started in Denver. The Brothers Redevelopment organization painted 100 houses a day from January through August. Sister notes: "I found out I had to do that too, in order to build my teams, get permissions, pick out the houses. We painted the houses of elderly people, 65 and over, who lived in their own home and were unable to have their house painted. By the fourth year, my team and I had painted 36 houses."[22]

Sister Mary Regis didn't just paint houses. She built them. Ten houses for ten families were built in partnership with HUD. Sweat equity was used to make the down payment. Not only did the work help families to purchase the homes but it also taught them a variety of painting skills and connected them to the property. Sister Mary Regis remarks: "They felt very connected to the house. It was their friend. They felt responsible for it. See, it wasn't like their rental where this belongs to someone else and we don't care."[23]

The work that Mary Regis describes was typical for the sisters ministering in property development. Small teams of sisters and partners would set out to a new property that needed rehabbing and work over the summer months, preparing the houses for habitation. Sister Jeanne Ward recalls learning to patch holes in walls while Sister Jeanne Christensen vividly remembers trying to figure out how to replace a dead water heater. Changing sinks, electrical wiring, plumbing, and even restringing old window blinds all went with the territory. They learned as they went, leaning on friends, contractors and experimentation to teach them. It was trial and error learning. Sister Jeanne Christensen passed on one trick she learned as she worked: "If you have to fix a peeling radiator, you use automotive paint. It can withstand the heat!"[24]

The lessons learned and passed on by the early circle of Mercy housing pioneers provided a landscape of what might be done. They embodied courage, ingenuity, chutzpah, daring, flexibility, and humility. No matter what was happening, they maintained a positive attitude. They were not afraid to try something new. Part of that positive spirit resided in each person, but another part was directly conveyed to them by Sister Terese Tracy herself. She believed in them, encouraged them, and gave them the latitude to experiment. Each one felt a link with her and knew she had their back. Sister Terese understood fully the need for communication and support. Recognizing the need for leadership to have face-to-face contact with those in the field, she moved the central offices to Denver in June 1983. The relocation made travel across Idaho, Colorado, Kansas, and Omaha easier for everyone.

By 1986, learnings from these initial years began to clarify the way forward. As Sister Mary Terese came to the end of her time at Mercy Housing, it was time to gather together those learnings. She had nurtured the growth of a new ministry, provided a path for addressing homelessness, gathered dedicated folks to help, and seen the fruit of her labors. Much good had been done but some models were not as sustainable as others, nor could they help as many people with the resources available.

Sister Mary Regis recognized that in her own work. "A single dwelling was really a luxury, when you think about it. Most of the people that we are helping as I see it now, are in townhouses, or in their apartment complexes."[25] To go forward, the sisters would once more have to read the signs of the times. Two questions had to be addressed: How do we find the monetary resources to fund this work going forward, and what changes do we need to implement to sustain the ministry? The urgency and way of addressing those issues was now placed in the hands of the second generation of Mercy Housing leaders.

For Your Reflection and Conversation

- In reading about the pioneer sisters' experiences during the early years of Mercy Housing, what most surprised you, impressed you, or challenged you?

- The founding sisters responded to the needs of their time. In what ways do these situations and challenges mirror those of contemporary time?

CHAPTER 4

FINDING THE MONEY ONE DOLLAR AT A TIME

When people discover that Mercy Housing has "participated in the development, preservation and/or financing of more than 48,200 affordable homes",[1] a frequent question is: "But where does the money come from to pay for all this?" That was a question facing the ministry from its beginning. Sister Terese knew that it would take skill, study, connections, negotiation, and lots of prayer to find the monies necessary to provide affordable housing for those desperate for a home of their own. Sister Jeanne Christensen puts it bluntly: "You can't be naïve. You have to learn how to negotiate. You want a good deal but they [lenders] want a good deal too."[2]

The learning curve was steep. Both Sister Terese and her successor Sister Lillian Murphy, a Sister of Mercy from the Burlingame community, who succeeded Sister Terese as Chief Executive Officer of Mercy Housing, had to master that curve. Although Sister Terese and Sister Lillian Murphy were top hospital administrators prior to their work at Mercy Housing, neither had experience in the complex world of funding affordable housing efforts. This they had to learn from the bottom up. Since both sisters were well versed in the dynamics of hospital boards, there was a vast network of connections and friends from the corporate sphere upon whom they could draw for advice and support. In this case, the saying, "It takes a village" was right on point.

In the initial years of Mercy Housing, the Sisters of Mercy began to address the money issue. The $500,000 set aside by the Omaha Province could not go very far. The first critical issue to be resolved was how to use the money set aside by the Province. One option was to help fund projects that other agencies working in affordable housing were undertaking. Another was to establish a fund from which interest could be used for a grant process to support such works. A third option, one encouraged by advisors like Jim Tomlinson, was to become owners of affordable housing properties themselves. Ownership won the day, bringing with it both challenges and opportunities.

The decision to own properties like the first five properties purchased in Idaho was made knowing that it required growing a pool of available monies which could be used to expand the ministry. The realization that more funds were needed was also fueled by the wisdom of a maxim frequently voiced in the Mercy community: "No mission, no margin; no margin, no mission." The way of mission was clear but the path to margin had to be shaped by trial and error.

The most familiar route to expanding funds was soliciting donations and grants, a process well known to Sister Terese Tracy and her associates. That process introduced a level of uncertainty about funding since grants had to be won through a competitive process. For donors, sudden deaths, economic downturns and unexpected situations can seriously impact contribution levels. Ultimately, such efforts provided an uncertain and limited pool of funding to support Mercy Housing's work.

The syndication process first used in Boise, Idaho, was another path. The syndication system depended on the ability to leverage Mercy Housing resources with those of other potential lenders. In the case of the Idaho properties, Mercy Housing partnered with DBSI, a real estate investment company. The DBSI company found investors willing to invest funds for low interest loans for monies to facilitate the purchase of the five Mercy Housing properties in Idaho. Over time these loans were repaid with interest. In the early '80s, interest rates were high, sometimes as high as 10% to 12%, so low interest loans were a God-sent.

Such a process works extremely well when values are congruent and goals are shared. One of the hard learnings from this partnership was that not every partnership is a good match. The values and vision of Mercy Housing and DBSI were divergent, one pastoral, one profit. As an investment company, DBSI was more focused on the profit outcome for investors while Mercy Housing saw the priority as the residents served. Jim Tomlinson, who also worked with DBSI, had a similar experience saying:

> This was an investment company—and imposed their management style on the sisters. They split with the sisters and bought the sisters out. They didn't want to spend money on the properties because they wanted to make a return on the investment."[3]

The variance in approach and values caused the sisters to dissolve their partnership with DBSI but taught them an important lesson. The new 1986 tax credit policy of the government provided a lucrative possibility for investors looking to get significant tax credits, but some prospective partners were not invested in affordable housing as a value. Future partnerships would be more intensely vetted to ensure a match of values and vision.

Since money was essential and with the development and management portions of Mercy Housing established by 1983, it was time to add a third segment to Mercy Housing, a branch dedicated to raising funds. McAuley Housing Foundation (now called Mercy Community Capital) filed its Articles of Incorporation and Bylaws in the state of Nebraska in February of 1983. With that complete, Mercy Housing now had a three-pronged model comprised of development, property management, and community capital as its working structure. While Mercy Housing itself focused on property development, Mercy Management Services was dedicated to resident well-being including the care of the properties themselves. Mercy Community Capital changed its name multiple times over the course of the next 40 years. Whether referred to as the Catherine McAuley Housing Foundation, the Mercy Loan Fund, or its current title Mercy Community Capital, it was always focused on raising and providing the financial resources needed to support affordable housing efforts. To avoid confusion, Mercy Community Capital will be used when speaking of the work of this aspect of Mercy Housing.

Mercy Community Capital didn't work exclusively on resources for Mercy Housing but linked to other agencies and groups working to provide housing for those in need. Patricia O'Roark explains: "We realized early on we did not only need to develop affordable housing ourselves, but we must support other nonprofits doing the same work with a shared goal for systemic change."[4] Sarah Smith, the first President of Mercy Community Capital, reflects: "There was always an understanding that Mercy Housing didn't have to be the only one doing the projects but that we could lend our influence and support to others aligned with us who were trying to do the same thing."[5]

After 40 years, Mercy Community Capital continues that mission. It captures that commitment on its website, saying:

> For over four decades, Mercy Community Capital has focused exclusively on funding affordable housing and essential community infrastructure projects that support affordable housing. By collaborating with socially responsible developers, Mercy Community Capital has helped finance the development of single and multifamily homes for rental and homeownership. These developments aid a variety of people, including low-income families and individuals, the working poor, seniors, farm workers, formerly homeless individuals and people with special needs.[6]

While it sounds so direct and straight-forward, the path to that reality was not simple. In the initial years of Mercy Housing, alternative investments were only beginning to be used by financial institutions. Tax credits, another way that is used to leverage funding, did not become available until 1986. What was emerging, however, was co-sponsorship agreements between religious orders, hospitals, and Catholic dioceses. To weave all this together while building the ministry took creativity, financial savvy, and a strong network of relationships. With the formation of Mercy Community Capital, Sister Terese looked for someone who possessed those qualities as well as a passion to help those in need. She found that someone in Sarah Smith.

Sarah joined Mercy Housing in August 1984. Sister Terese first met Sarah at Colorado Rural Housing Corporation where Sister Terese was attending a meeting. It was the beginning of a rich and long relationship. Six months later, Sister Terese invited Sarah to apply for the role of President of Mercy Community

Capital. Excited by the mission and vision of the organization, she said yes! It was a fortuitous partnering. Sarah brought a creative and innovative vision to acquiring capital. Sister Regis Leahy says: "Sarah Smith was the financial genius, because she had an entrepreneurial approach to borrowing money from different religious orders and working from the interest of that money. That was how we acquired property."[7]

When you try to imagine the environment of someone who is charged with raising millions of dollars, you would never imagine the type of office that awaited Mercy Community Capital's new President. It was really borrowed space offered to her by Mercy Hospital in Denver. The day she arrived she found a desk, file cabinet, telephone, and the Articles of Incorporation and By-Laws of the new subsidiary.[8] It was a no-frills deal just like all early offices of Mercy Housing. From there Sarah would go to work.

Before Sarah Smith assumed the role of President of Mercy Community Capital, then called the Catherine McAuley Housing Foundation (CMHF), Sister Terese had already begun visiting various bishops to see if they were interested in supporting Mercy Housing by providing funds through loans or donations. In April and May of 1983, she visited Bishop Tafoya of Pueblo, Colorado, Archbishop Sheehan of Omaha, Nebraska, and Archbishop Casey of Denver, Colorado. Building on common values and longstanding personal or community relationships, Sister Terese was committed to establishing a culture of collaboration and partnership.

In the meanwhile, the task of helping other agencies be successful and supported wasn't neglected. Patricia O'Roark and Sister Marilyn Ross worked together on trying to get insurance companies to invest in Holy Name Housing Corporation Project in Omaha, NE. Holy Name Housing Corporation aligned with the values and work of Mercy Housing and was in great need of funding for its work. In 1983, Mercy Community Capital began actively supporting the independent Holy Name Housing Corporation monetarily, and Sister Marilyn started her work there. Both she and Patricia O'Roark were instrumental in obtaining over $1 million for a revolving loan fund for homeowners in North Omaha.[9]

A critical source of early capital came from low interest loans. Obtaining such funding involved seeking out religious communities, faith communities and dioceses, healthcare systems, banks, and corporations who were committed to making life better for those who were poor. Mercy Housing would invite such entities to partner with it by lending the ministry monies for five years at a minimal rate of interest. Such loans provided both the lender and the recipient a means of addressing such critical concerns as excessive rental burdens for families, unsafe housing conditions, lack of affordable housing, and homelessness in all its forms. The impact of low interest investments was just beginning to be understood by communities and faith-rooted groups as a means to make a real difference in the lives of those who were struggling. In a sense, such investments allowed the group to make an impact they could not achieve on their own. Low interest investments became an essential component of the funding mix of Mercy Housing. Today such loans still play a vital role in funding new projects.

A publication of MHI in 1987 states that: "The Foundation was focused on the financing and funding of worthy projects."[10] The summary overview of the organization goes on to say:

> The Foundation has been structured to achieve this
> by securing low and no interest loans and donations
> from a diversified range of sources and channeling
> them into well-conceived projects. The Foundation

uses loans as its main mode of assistance to projects. Grants may be provided by CMHF depending upon the availability of funds and the ability of the grant money to leverage significant additional funds. The Foundation also takes a proactive role in seeking outside resources for selected projects and promoting innovative and effective financing arrangements.[11]

The spirit of collaborative action alive in Mercy Housing today was present from the beginning. Between 1986 and 1989, Mercy Community Capital was able to provide over $1.4 million for housing and community development initiatives in seven states. Just how effective it was in building connections and relationships is seen in the list of supporters listed in Mercy Housing's 1989 publication of "Addressing the Housing Crisis." The list included over 80 organizations that had supported Mercy Housing's work, including religious communities like the Adrian Dominicans, the Christian Brothers, the Redemptorist Fathers of the St. Louis Province, the Sisters of Loretto, multiple Mercy provinces and communities, several archdioceses, and 19 health-care institutions. The supporters were not limited to Catholic organizations. They also included groups like Ralston Purina Trust Fund, Raskob Foundation, Arthur Anderson & Co., U.S. Farmers Home Administration, the City of Omaha, and Hallmark Cards to name a few.[12] Within fifteen years, that number had almost doubled!

By 2001, the strength of the Mercy Community Capital Foundation had grown significantly. For every dollar invested in it, $7 of affordable housing was developed. By making the loans that traditional financial institutions preferred to decline, MCC provided close to $91 million in loans and leveraged another

$650 million in affordable housing financing resulting in more than 900 units of affordable housing over 20 states.[13] By 2020 that had increased to $420 million in loans and another $2.76 billion dollars in the pipeline for more development.[14] Stefanie Joy, President of Mercy Community Capital, considers the growth of its capacity to be one of the most significant successes of the last decade. She notes that in 2012 MCC had $44 million available for loans. In 2025 that amount was $138 million, an incredible expansion.[15]The impact was formidable. Mercy Community Capital had helped to create or preserve 48,400 units of housing, leveraged 9.2 billion dollars over 45 states plus Puerto Rico.[16]

The credibility earned by Mercy Community Capital was recognized by the Department of the Treasury as early as 2000, when it designated it as a Community Development Financial Institution. This designation allowed Mercy Community Capital to access both financial and technical assistance. This certification was a significant factor in expanding the loan capacity of MCC. The Financial Assistance awards could be used for lending capital, loan loss reserves, capital reserves, operations, and development services as long as matching funds from a non-federal source could be provided.

Sometimes monies loaned by Mercy Community Capital allow a project the final help needed to come to completion. That was the case with Valley Crisis Center in Nampa, Idaho. The center was the only domestic violence shelter in Idaho's Canyon County and six other surrounding counties. Mercy Housing Idaho had agreed to take on the work of developer and sponsor for the property. Although federal block grants and a Community Development Block Grant had secured more than $800,000 for the project, $150,000 more was needed to make it happen. The loan from Mercy Community Capital provided those monies at an extremely low rate by securing an alternative investment from

Catholic Health Initiatives, one of Mercy Housing's Strategic Health Care Partnerships. By 1999, Valley Crisis Center opened its new doors and by 2001 was providing 25% of the domestic violence services in the State of Idaho.[17]

The Valley Crisis Center experience highlights the role of alternative investments. This form of investing was in its infancy when Mercy Housing was born but became a vital element in its practice. By tapping into its collaborative partners, especially healthcare systems, the loan fund was able to provide capital needed by small agencies and non-profit groups. The loaned capital provided other smaller scale affordable housing efforts vital resources. Such loans allowed them to succeed in their efforts. Interest rates were low, around 1% to 3%, and the loans were payable over time. None of this was easy, however. It demanded time and energy to build relationships and connections of trust.

Just how complicated funding affordable housing projects could be is described by Sister Diane Clyne RSM. Sister Diane, like many of the early sisters came from the field of education but was drawn to helping the vulnerable who needed housing. She was a friend of Sister Lillian who invited her to join in the early work of Mercy Housing in California. Sister Diane came to Mercy Housing before it put into place an internship in housing of its own. Twenty-three sisters went through the program giving living witness to the values it espoused. Eleven of the sister interns would become Mercy Housing employees. Internship was not Sister Diane's path. Before becoming part of Mercy Housing, Sister Diane had experience in housing through her work at the Office of Shared Housing in the Diocese of San Jose, California. There she matched seniors with persons who could live with them, allowing seniors to continue to live in their own homes, as well as providing shelter for the companions.

The Sisters of Mercy of Burlingame, of which Sister Diane was a member, were also involved in the Sanctuary Movement of the 1980s. The Sanctuary movement was a religious and political response to the plight of Central American refugees coming to the U.S. to escape the violence of their countries. Over 500 religious and charitable communities housed these refugees as a response to human need, but the reality also pointed to the need for more housing. By declaring themselves official "sanctuaries," the communities challenged governmental policy that made asylum difficult for those fleeing civil disruption, while committing to providing shelter, protection, material goods, and often legal advice to Central American refugees. These were the experiences that Sister Diane brought to her new work as a "housing developer." As Sister Diane notes: "It gave me a taste of the need."[18] Once more it was "learn as you go."

The complexity of funding was on full display with her first Mercy Housing assignment as developer for the Baker Street project in San Francisco. St. Mary's Hospital had undertaken the rehab of the abandoned Southern Pacific Railroad Hospital to provide 100 housing units for seniors, but all the outbuildings on the site, including its historic powerhouse, were left untouched. Sister Diane's project, called Mercy Family Plaza, was designed for family housing with a view to providing multi-generational communities by connecting the senior residents living at the renovated hospital with a neighborhood of families around them. The outbuildings would provide housing for 36 families.

Like today, Sister Diane estimates that eight to ten streams of funding went into this single undertaking. Each stream of funding had its own demands, timelines, limitations, and goals. Since the powerhouse was designated a historical building, there were special tax credits available. The caveat was that the historical preservation of the building had to be honored. City and county monies were also fed into the project, some open-ended and some time-limited. HUD provided Section 8 funding; other funds came through alternative investments, businesses seeking tax credits, and loans from healthcare or business entities. All these sources had to be woven together, requirements integrated into planning, and providers kept in the communication loop.

Mercy Family Plaza, San Francisco, was not the only property that needed a significant stream of funding. All major projects and communities found that only through a wide coalition could hope become a reality. The 2009 opening of Piñon Terrace, a 66-unit property in Durango, Colorado, is another good example of such collaboration. In this instance, Mercy Housing was supported by the Southern Ute Indian Tribe Growth Fund and Mercy Regional Medical Center. Piñon Terrace stands on land donated by Mercy Regional Medical Center. This was significant because the medical center's parent organization, Catholic Health Initiative, was committed to partnering with Mercy Housing to increase access to affordable housing and healthcare in the communities they served. The Piñon Terrace property was one of three such initiatives serving more than 350 Durangoans.

Mercy Regional Medical Center and the Southern Ute Indian Tribe Growth Fund were not the only supporters. Like all Mercy Housing projects, additional funding streams and support were needed. In this case, that included an additional twelve groups which played a significant role in bringing this new property to completion: the Boettcher Foundation, the City of Durango, JP Morgan Chase, JP Morgan Capital Corporation, the Colorado Division of Housing, the Colorado Housing and Finance Authority, the Durango Area Association of Realtors, the Federal Home Loan Bank of Chicago, GRVP, LLC, and the Affordable

Housing Trust.[19] The culture of collaboration fostered by both Sister Terese Tracy and Sister Lillian Murphy was essential in weaving together diverse entities for every project undertaken by Mercy Housing.

Money streams were essential for providing needed housing, but so was money in hand when it came to "closing" the deal. At the time of signing the final papers for a project, Sister Lillian, then President of Mercy Housing, needed to be able to hand over the required monies. Another anecdote from Sister Diane Clyne makes that very clear. Sister Lillian had come to San Francisco to turn over the needed closure monies for Mercy Family Plaza at the time of completion. There was only one problem. The bank holding the monies would not release the funds until they held them for three days. That would make the closure fall apart. Sister Lillian quickly dispatched Sister Diane to convince the bank to release the monies. She was not to return without the funds. With tenacity, Sister Diane went through a long process of moving from teller to teller, person to person, up the line of authority until she finally reached a person with the authority to release the funds.[20] Accepting "No" was not an option. Pure perseverance, determination, and lots of prayer won the day.

Grants, like that awarded in 2009 to Intercommunity Mercy Housing in Tacoma, Washington, were also an important part of funding. Intercommunity Mercy Housing, founded in 1992 through a collaboration of four religious communities in the Northwest, originally was called Intercommunity Housing. Since its name has changed over time, for purposes of clarity we will use its current name Mercy Housing Northwest throughout the rest of the story. The hope of the communities was to significantly act to reduce homelessness in their area of service. After its merger with Mercy Housing in 1992, the ministry was able to deepen its impact. An award from HUD for $8.2 million covered almost one-third of the development costs to construct New Tacoma, a 73-apartment complex for seniors. Specially designed apartments with such things as grab bars, wide corridors, and roll-in showers allowed new senior residents to be safe and independent. The location of New Tacoma was near enough to other Mercy family housing to allow for intergenerational learning, field trips to local attractions, volunteers opportunities, and easy access to clinics. Such things as gardening, classes, and wellness programs were provided, all in the service of creating an environment of care and empowerment for the residents.[21]

Monies did not always just go to build or rehab large buildings. Sometimes it was needed for smaller but impactful undertakings like a Self-Help Program in Magic Valley, Idaho, funded in 2009. Approximately 100 families there have been able to build and buy their homes through Mercy Housing Idaho's Self-Help Homeowners Program. Ten families joined together as a build team and helped each other, with each team member committing to 35 hours a week of sweat equity. Their work provided their down payment on their future home and added equity to their homes. Once completed, the USDA Rural Development offers them low-interest loans to pay the remaining costs. Mercy Housing also secured grants from both the Idaho Housing and Finance Association and the Federal Home Loan Bank of Seattle.[22]

Over the first 40 years of Mercy Housing's work, lines of equity, use of tax credits, bridge loans, land donations from entities that wanted to address the critical need for affordable housing, and a variety of modes which provided needed monies were not always constant. To be used effectively, Mercy Housing staff had to be vigilant in monitoring changes in governmental policy, criteria for receiving grants from such agencies as Fannie Mae, changes in tax credit rules, or dates when such credits expire. It was one thing to be awarded the grant or tax credit. It was another to be able to comply with all its requirements and deadlines. Two things were constant: agility in responding to the opportunities that presented themselves and the need for a long view. Not all deals or opportunities were in the best interest of the ministry.

Financial acuity demands more than skills in obtaining monies. It requires that you use them wisely and strategically. In the beginning of Mercy Housing, internal monies were quite limited; in fact, many of the early sister pioneers initially worked without salaries. Being careful with monies came naturally to the sisters who took to heart the saying of Catherine McAuley:

> Although I should be simple as a Dove, I must also be prudent as a Serpent; and, since there is very little good can be accomplished, or evil avoided, without the aid of money, we must look after it in small as well as in great matters.[23]

While in the beginning the Sisters of Mercy underwrote the salaries of sisters working at Mercy Housing, as the ministry developed there was a need to increase fiscal discipline. In Sister Geraldine Hoyler CSC, Sister Lillian found just the right person to provide that discipline. Mercy Housing was just ten years old and it was time to take stock of its organizational structure.

Sister Geraldine was a former CFO of a healthcare system prior to her joining the Mercy Housing staff. Initially she came as a developer, but that role lasted only three weeks because, by the end of week two, Sister Lillian was reorganizing. She wanted to place development oversight, social support services, and property management into Mercy Services Corporation. Sister Geraldine said: "I could do that." Two weeks later that is exactly what she was doing.[24]

What Sister Geraldine put in place was really asset management and she did it by establishing a disciplined way of monitoring expenses.

> But from then on [1992] until I left at the end of October of 1996, I signed every single cheque on every single property and that was our internal control. It was my second look review at that to try to manage the cash flow and who would get paid and when they would get paid. And it took a lot of time to sign all those cheques but it was a management tool.[25]

In her office at Mercy Services Corporation, she was joined by Kathleen Brownlee and Marla Brant. Together they were able to organize in a way that ensured everyone knew they weren't getting into deals that couldn't be managed, especially tax credit deals. To stay fiscally sound, you had to make difficult choices. One learning was that scattered-site housing was not feasible. It was too difficult to manage fiscally, and the Kansas scattered-site houses had to be turned over to others.

That learning was reinforced in Mercy Housing Northwest's work with Cobble Knoll, a struggling set of 30 properties Mercy Housing purchased with public funding. Its owner could not continue, and affordable housing options were at risk of being lost. The properties, following the I-5 corridor, were spread throughout Washington, many in rural areas. It was a challenging deal for Mercy, explained Charles Wehrwein, Senior Vice President of Mercy Housing, Inc., appearing before a Committee on Financial Services and a Subcommittee on Housing and Community Opportunity in the U.S. House of Representatives' hearing. While meeting the need to preserve affordable housing for its residents, Cobble Knoll was also a pilot to see if focusing on rural housing was feasible. He said that Mercy Housing's goals in acquiring the Cobble Knoll portfolio were as follows:

- To preserve and strengthen these 926 units of deeply affordable housing for the poor rural seniors and families who depend on this resource;

- To test if rural preservation could be done on a large and efficient scale;

- To attempt to structure the new ownership so that it was economically viable for a non-profit with a long-term ownership horizon; and

- To call out the tools that are useful in making rural preservation happen at scale, and the impediments in pursuing this strategy.[26]

Mercy Housing also learned that size matters. A property that was too small was both difficult to fund and difficult to support. As Sister Geraldine talked with all the developers, some guidelines began to emerge, and these led to a strategic plan. As she explains, you couldn't do everything:

> Getting enough money in the project to begin with was challenging ... and you couldn't do that with small ones. Concentrating your units so you could manage them. Trying to hang on to people's services so you weren't paying for the cost of the services was important fiscally.[27]

This was a serious concern since the ministry was growing significantly. As Mercy Housing added new co-sponsors, requests for affordable housing initiatives were coming from multiple directions. Fannie Mae, as well as advocacy groups, were also asking for expansion to the East Coast. All of this meant that planning and structuring for mission effectiveness took on a new urgency.

It would be easy to assume that the expertise gained in the first 15 years was the way it would always be. In some ways that is true. The mission and values never changed, but between 1981 and 2006, there were some other significant changes. When the pioneer sisters started providing affordable housing, they simply responded to need. After 25 years, it was evident that there needed to be a course correction. The learnings from the Cobble Knoll undertaking were significant as Mercy Housing, in 2005, looked at what was needed to have optimum efficiency from its structures, processes, and policies.

Steve Spears, CFO of Mercy Housing from 2012 to 2022, identified changes in HUD funding as a factor in changing the ways in which monies were found to finance both the operating and development costs, such as funding projects in the pipeline or constructing the buildings themselves. Prior to 2012, HUD had given large grants to build developments but it discontinued that funding. Spears remembers how challenging it was to fill the gap and recognizes that, even now, that gap still exists. Without government funding, there isn't enough capital available to build as much affordable housing as is needed.[28]

Colin Morgan-Cross, Vice President for Real Estate Development, identifies the expansion of local support as one of the key differences he sees between the earlier funding streams and the present day. It is less national and more local. That dynamic reinforced the need to collaborate, collaborate, collaborate. It is now all about bonding with partners and collaborators as well as an intensive focus on the community itself playing a role in what is built and what services are provided.[29]

Mercy Greenbrae, located on the former Marylhurst Campus in Lake Oswego, Oregon, reflects those local ties. Opened in 2024, its listing of partners includes nine entities: Oregon Department of Housing and Community Services; Oregon Metro; the Housing Authority of Clackamas County; Oregon Multifamily Energy Program; Energy Trust of Oregon; Sisters of the Holy Names of Jesus and Mary; Key Bank (construction lender and long-term lender); Key Community Development Corporation (Tax Credit investor); and Mercy Housing, Inc. The funders were almost all local.

Another change Colin Morgan-Cross sees, especially in the Northwest, is the emergence of Tech Companies as partners. Recognizing their contribution to the housing shortages, especially in the sphere of affordable housing, groups like the Paul Allen Foundation, Micro Soft Loan Fund, and Amazon funding have all lent their support and resources to non-profits addressing the housing crisis.[30]

The combination of mission, collaboration, community involvement, and a proven record of providing what you promise to provide are all essential in attracting donors and partners to the work of affordable housing. This was vital in the growth of the ministry. Steve Spears explains that, in bridging the gap, Mercy Housing directly sought the investment of banks through syndication. That was only possible because Mercy had grown big enough and sophisticated enough to attract their attention. That way, Mercy worked directly with banks to achieve better pricing.[31]

Once more the essential task of building strong relationships came into play. As Spears explains: "You are always one phone call away from losing a line of credit that is essential for the project. Being transparent, having both strong lines of communication and relationships of trust are vital."[32] In light of that reality, Spears began to hold twice-yearly meetings with the banking community. The first meeting shared what was happening, what was planned, the good and the not so good alike. The second meeting was storytelling, allowing the banks to see what they had achieved by partnering and all the good they had helped to bring about. They could take pride in their partnership.

One internal change implemented by Spears and his collaborators was a strengthening of Mercy Housing's cash reserve policies. Recognizing the fragility of credit lines, he worked to have sufficient cash reserves to meet any unexpected shortfalls. First, he simply asked for a nickel out of every dollar but ultimately was able to make sure that there were sufficient cash reserves to finance 100% of Mercy Housing's debt. By 2014, the yearly budget allotted $2 million to pay down debt and another $2 million to strengthen cash reserves. Making the internal structure strong was not a goal in itself. It was to strengthen the organization to better do its mission.[33]

Sister Lillian believed that In order to carry out any mission, no matter what the mission is, you have to maintain your infrastructure and you have to maintain your people and to do both sides. You have to be true to whatever you present as your "public face" to keep the integrity of the organization and to keep your ability to do what you need to do in your public forum.

> And so, from my perspective, it's always about infrastructure and you're always having to reevaluate and restructure your infrastructure because the world changes around you and you change internally. Understand your mission, understand the components of your mission and make sure you structure yourself to do it.[34]

In the vision of Sister Lillian Murphy, mission and business went hand-in-hand. The success of one depended on the health and well-being of the other. As she put it: "The mission is the umbrella over everything that we do. There are some qualitative aspects, some quantitative, and we need to pay attention to both. And I think that has been a core of what we've been doing since we started."[35]

Sister Lillian was also keenly aware of the impact that philanthropy can have on the works of mercy. She knew that to ask others to support the work of Mercy Housing through their philanthropic donations, not only provided needed monies but also needed advocates and connectors. It gave donors a chance to make a significant difference in the lives of others and of society itself. Such efforts were not just local, they expanded to encompass national and regional and regional opportunities. Ismael Guerrero, Mercy Housing's Chief Executive Officer, points out that in the early years the mindset was "no margin, no mission." Staying focused on the sustainability of real estate development activities and a strong philanthropic program are critical because "more margin means more mission."[36]

In describing Mercy Housing's strong philanthropic program, you might say that it is donor driven and works inspired. The founding sisters believed that the work done was the witness prompting others to join in the efforts. They didn't design a big marketing campaign. Mercy marketing consisted of excellence at every level of the ministry and the witness of an environment of respect and compassion for all community members whether resident, staff or administrator. That would draw others into the endeavor. A great example of how that works is MacKenzie Scott's $25 million donation to Mercy Housing through the Yield Giving Foundation. She was drawn to work that Mercy Housing was doing, had it thoroughly vetted by her organization and ultimately awarded the generous grant. It was the work that grabbed her interest and her heart. The proven record of Mercy Housing provided the trust-base that monies would be used wisely and prudently. Such trust-based donations are the result of building relationships through transparency and communication.

Today the grant from the Yield Giving Foundation provides needed monies for a variety of programs that would not be possible with such funding: training for front line fundraising, an internal Community Impact Fund, exploration of ways of partnering in a financially sustainable manner with healthcare systems and many more. Donations at the national level are divided among all the regions unless restricted by donors.

Sometimes Mercy Housing donors are not individuals but corporations. At both the national and regional levels, donations can be non-restricted, meaning that the monies go to needs designated by Mercy Housing, or they can be designated for special needs. An example of such donations would be Walmart's focus on providing monies for food banks.

At the regional or local level, philanthropy takes a variety of forms, everything from gala events which result in high profile exposure for corporate donors to small initiatives like that of the Sisters at Holy Spirit Parish in Sacramento. Understanding the critical need for bedding and kitchen supplies that would be needed by the 134 new residents moving into St. Claire at Capitol Park, the sisters sent a single flyer to the parish asking for new or good condition items of bedding or kitchen supplies. The need was explained in the Sunday announcements. Some parishioners took extra flyers home to distribute in their neighborhood. Others invited friends from other areas to join in the effort. Just one small invitation resulted in three large truckloads of supplies for St. Clarie's, enough bedding for every room and ample kitchen supplies. As one parishioner put it: "It was wonderful to be able to do something concrete to help those in need."

The efforts at St. Claire were concrete and immediate but future needs must also be addressed. Connie Rule, Mercy Housing Chief of Strategic Partnerships, shares that endowment donations are really legacy ones which carry the vision and compassion of the donor into the future. They have a lasting impact. One of the valuable projects funded by the MacKenzie Scott donation is a multi-year endowment campaign which seeks to raise $25,000,000 for Mercy Housing's long-term sustainability and enduring impact. Already $8 million has been raised for the effort. For Mercy Housing, every philanthropic donation gives donors the opportunity to respond to present needs thereby making a difference in the lives of vulnerable people as well as a chance to leave a legacy gift that continues to change persons lives well into the future.

The challenge to adapt to changing realities internally and externally remains constant. Over its 40-plus-year history, Mercy Housing has consistently adapted to each new wave of change. Some were small and incremental; some were transformative. One of the greatest challenges as Mercy Housing matured as a ministry was also one of its great blessings, the emergence of co-sponsorship. In 1989, the first two co-sponsors, the Auburn and Burlingame Mercy regional communities, each contributed $500,000 to Mercy Housing, providing additional leverage for loans and funding. While alternative investments were built on mission and relationships, co-sponsorship demanded more. It required that the founding community, the Mercy Omaha Province, be open to sharing responsibility for the oversight and mission of the ministry with their new co-sponsors. That decision led Mercy Housing into a future its pioneer sisters never envisioned.

For Your Reflection and Conversation

- Mercy Housing has had to face financial challenges over the course of its history. To remain fiscally sound, it has had to withdraw from some endeavors like scattered-site housing. Those who believed in that model found this difficult. What changes have you found difficult over your association with Mercy Housing? In what ways have you seen those changes bring blessings or regrets?

- Within a year of its foundation, Mercy Housing established Mercy Community Capital to assist small non-profits who had similar goals and values. Forty years later, how do you see this element of Mercy Housing as vital to its mission?

PHOTO GALLERY

Image of Catherine McAuley (artist Cloy Kent, 1981), courtesy of Mercy Archives, Sisters of Mercy of the Americas

The House of Mercy on Baggot Street (artist Sister Maura Barga), courtesy of Mercy Archives, Sisters of Mercy of the Americas

The Sisters of Mercy Generalate,
courtesy of Mercy Archives, Sisters
of Mercy of the Americas

Patricia O'Roark

Long-range planning meeting, 1981

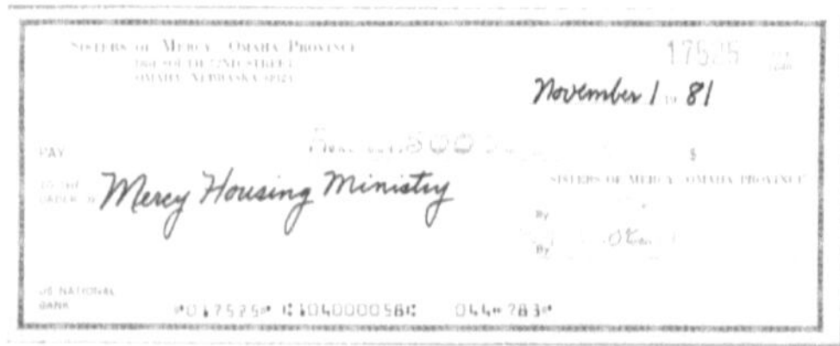

The $500,000 check that started it all

*Sister Terese Tracy in the doorway of
Washington Park Townhouses Idaho, 1985*

*Left to right: A Sister of Mercy of Omaha, Patricia
O'Roark, Jim Tomlinson, Sister Terese Tracy,
Sister Vera O'Connor, Sister Jean Beste, Sister
Stella Neill, and Sister Jeanne Ward, 1985*

*Sister Terese Tracy and
Sister Lillian Murphy after
Sister Lillian interviewed for
the position of chief executive
officer, 1987*

*Grand Cascade
Apartments in American
Falls, Idaho, 1983*

*Sister Lillian Murphy and children at Decatur Place
Apartments in Denver, Colorado*

*Sarah Smith, first President of Mercy
Community Capital*

*The founding communities of
Intercommunity Housing at the time of the
merger with Mercy Housing*

*Sister Diane Clyne
looking out the window
of Mercy Family Plaza*

*Jane Graf, former President
and Chief Executive Officer of
Mercy Housing*

*Anita, the first resident of Mercy
Terrace, moving in*

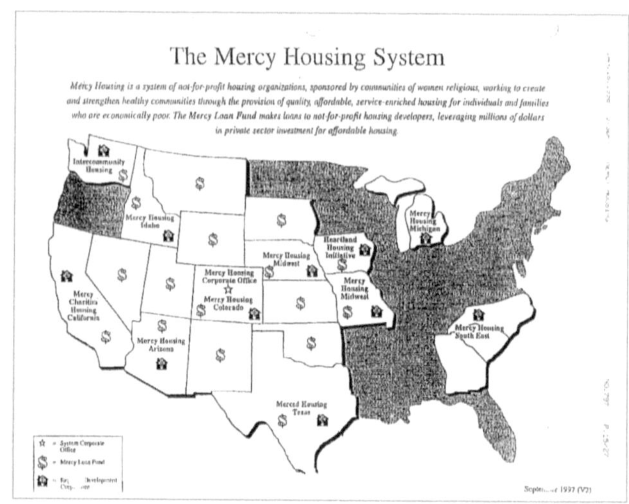

The Mercy Housing system, 1998

Constructing New Tacoma Senior
Apartments, Tacoma, Washington

Aerial view of Mercy Magnuson Place on grand opening day, Seattle, Washington

First hospital in Savannah, Georgia, that trained African American nurses and doctors, redeveloped into Heritage Place

Sunnydale resident standing in front of 1940s barracks that had fallen into disrepair and were redeveloped by Mercy Housing

The Sunnydale development, 290 Malosi Street, San Francisco, California

Lofts on Arthington in Chicago, Illinois, before renovations

*Lofts on Arthington
in Chicago, Illinois,
after renovations*

*Mr. McClinton standing in
front of Savannah Gardens in
Savannah, Georgia*

*Young dancer at the 9th and Navajo
groundbreaking celebration in
Denver, Colorado*

Chair yoga at a senior apartment community

Community Connect at Lofts on Arthington in Chicago, Illinois

Homework Club at Sterling Meadows in Bellingham, Washington

Food pantry at Mercy Magnuson Park in Seattle, Washington

Michael Boyd with grandchild

Mercy Housing President and Chief Executive Officer Ismael Guerrero in front of Franconia Apartments in Denver, Colorado

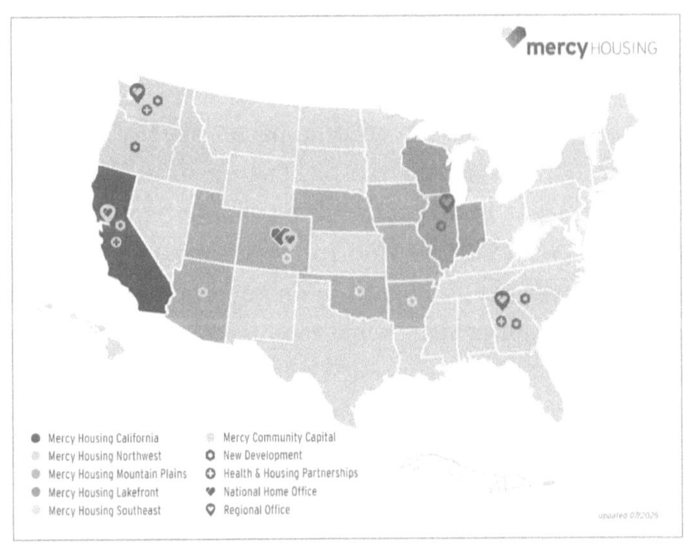

Mercy Housing national map, 2025

CHAPTER 5

BETTER TOGETHER

In American mythology, there are many different images that capture the American Spirit. There is the image of the cowboy, a loner who acts on his own, or the image of the self-made person who didn't need anyone's help to succeed. These images have captured our imaginations for decades but other compelling images exist that present a different reality: one of a pioneer community barn-raising when neighbors come together to provide what is needed, or the quilting bees, which not only foster community but witness the truth that things work better when folks join together in an undertaking. These two latter images capture the spirit of Mercy Housing from its very beginning. No undertaking was ever the fruit of one person or one agency. It was that conviction which fueled the move to co-sponsorship.

In 1989, when Mercy Housing first ventured down the path of co-sponsorship with the Mercy Auburn and Burlingame regional communities, co-sponsorship was a relatively new concept. It was just emerging among religious communities accustomed to doing things on their own. By the late '80s, religious communities began to bring healthcare systems together, to share ministries. Then, in 1991, Sisters of Mercy across the Americas formed a single Institute, the Sisters of Mercy of the Americas. The Mercy Omaha Province was part of that movement. It wasn't just a structural change. It was a coming together for life and mission.

For some regions, forming one Mercy Institute was an impetus to explore the possibility of co-sponsoring Mercy Housing. Sister Richard Mary Burke, then President of Mercy's St. Louis Region, puts it this way: "Our challenge was to see how we could help the regional community grow in an awareness and connection Institute-wide. That was really the thinking behind looking into Mercy Housing. Where could we become more active outside our regional community boundary?"[1]

The initial idea of inviting other communities to join in the housing ministry came from Sister Vera O'Connell RSM. Sister Norita Cooney remembers:

> It was Sister Vera that I think had the idea to do that and she saw it as a way of extending the ministry of housing. And for Vera, the ministry was always the top priority. If she felt there was any way that we could make ministries more viable she'd do anything she felt we needed to do in order to do that. And she was the one who first introduced the idea of looking at co-sponsorship.[2]

Sister Norita went on to explain that the concept of sponsorship and co-sponsorship was evolving in healthcare. It wasn't limited to the housing ministry. It was a trend, one that was seen as an opportunity for expanding ministry and providing needed services to an extent not possible for a single sponsor.

The movement toward co-sponsorship was not solely prompted by a decision to share resources for the sake of the mission. Sister

Norita identified another factor as highly significant. "Probably one of the biggest factors that's been influencing [co-sponsorship] is the decrease in the number of sisters."[3] The decrease in membership meant having governing bodies composed solely of sisters was not sustainable in the future. A new model was needed. The evolution and development of sponsorship and co-sponsorship meant that it became normative for responsibilities to be assumed by boards comprised jointly of religious and laity. It was the primary responsibility of the religious community to see that the charism of the community within that particular ministry was carried out, nourished, and that it continued to be the guiding and animating touchstone.

Sister Pat Eck, a member of the Sisters of Bon Secour Community, describes the evolving nature of co-sponsorship this way. "I think one of the major expectations that we had was just to be in relationship with other religious leaders and to be in a co-sponsorship. Knowing that sponsorship was changing, and the way organizations were influenced was changing, we just wanted to be a part of that."[4]

When Sister Terese Tracy left Mercy Housing to serve in Mercy Community leadership, Sister Lillian Murphy, her successor, seized the moment to share the Mercy Housing story and seek the involvement of other religious communities as co-sponsors. As a sister of the west, Sister Lillian was a personal friend and colleague of leaders in both the Auburn and Burlingame Mercy communities. It was not surprising that she approached both groups with a vision of what could happen.

Co-sponsorship was not new to either community. Both had engaged in a lengthy process of combining their healthcare systems to create Catholic Healthcare West. That experience of co-sponsorship was initiated in 1986. Simultaneously with other

Mercy groups, they were also engaging in the process of becoming a single Institute. There was a lot on their plate!

The seeds for collaboration had been planted several years before Sister Lillian approached both communities. Sister Terese Marie Perry remembers:

> I was inspired when I read a little bulletin that Omaha put out about forming Mercy Housing with a picture of Terese Tracy. And I finally got to see who Terese Tracy was because I had heard about her for so long that I was so inspired when I read that. I thought, I wish we had thought about that.[5]

What attracted Sister Terese Marie was the corporate nature of the commitment made by the Omaha Province. Sister Terese Marie went on to explain: "We had a direction statement at that time that asked and challenged us to look at ministries for the poor. We were focusing on individual ministries, but Mercy Housing was a corporate ministry."[6] She recalled the words of Sister Maura Power, then President of the Auburn Mercy Community: "We can do it better together than alone."[7]

For Sister Maura Power, her connection with Mercy Housing emerged from a long-standing relationship with members of the Mercy Omaha Province, then serving in Red Bluff and Grass Valley. Through informal sharing, she had heard about the Omaha Sisters' commitment to a corporation housing ministry. The seeds for co-sponsoring Mercy Housing were planted in her imagination as early as 1985 during a visit with Sister Vera O'Connor. Sister Maura remembers that Sister Vera suggested that the Auburn Community might like to join with Omaha in Mercy Housing. Sister Maura notes that the timing was bad. The formation of Catholic Healthcare West and of the Mercy Institute claimed all the region's energy.[8]

The idea was not forgotten, only postponed, because homelessness never decreased. By 1988, the idea of co-sponsoring Mercy Housing found a place on the Burlingame Chapter's agenda. The proposal was that the Burlingame community join with Omaha and Auburn in sponsoring Mercy Housing. In the spring of 1989, the Burlingame Chapter unanimously adopted the proposal.

Meanwhile, in Auburn, the movement to co-sponsorship was also progressing. Having completed the formation of Catholic Healthcare West and with the movement to Institute well underway, the time seemed right to revisit the idea of co-sponsoring Mercy Housing. Sister Lillian came to talk with the Auburn leadership team shortly after the Burlingame Chapter and, prompted by the action of the Burlingame community, an identical proposal was presented to the Auburn sisters. Sister Maura remembers that there was strong support for the proposal.

> Over the years many sisters said they would always remember that special meeting we had on Mercy Housing. And when the proposal was made that we give a half million dollars to Mercy Housing, everybody kind of gasped at the moment. But we had it … Some of the sisters said they just felt so thrilled to think that we would do that. Spend that money for the Works of Mercy, especially for housing for the low income and the needy. So, there was great enthusiasm about it as well.[9]

For Mercy Housing, the reality of a new governance structure, that of co-sponsorship, provided a model that would replicate itself over the coming years as more religious communities signed on as co-sponsors. Each brought with it a contribution of $500,000, allowing the capital resources of the ministry to expand and provide additional leverage for new endeavors. Communities brought more than money, however. They provided a network of connections and a pool of leaders for projects going forward.

The Auburn and Burlingame communities might have been the first co-sponsors but they were not the last. Between 1989 and 2003, the total number of co-sponsors grew to include 13 co-sponsoring religious communities. In 1993, the Sisters of St. Joseph of Peace, Western Province, and the Sisters of Mercy, Cedar Rapids, both joined as co-sponsors. Next came the Daughters of Charity, West, and the Sisters of St. Joseph of Orange. They were rapidly followed by the Sisters of Bon Secours, the Daughters of Charity, Central, and the Sisters of Mercy, St. Louis. Before the end of the century, in 1999, the Daughters of Charity, East Central joined the circle of sponsors. Still, they were not done. The Sisters of Mercy of Chicago and those of Connecticut were the last two groups to join as co-sponsors in 2003.

Often, new corporate members were anxious to have Mercy Housing address the lack of affordable housing in their specific area of the country. It was need that motivated. Sister Pat Eck put it this way:

> This need seems so obvious, especially from our take as being in healthcare. The importance of providing stable housing for those in need, so that they have the opportunity to have wellness and health. That stable housing is just an essential component of that, so it made sense for us, moving in that direction.[10]

Initially a small regional presence, Mercy Housing grew to be a national leader in affordable housing through the advocacy and involvement of its co-sponsors.

Since new religious sponsors were spread out throughout the United States, Mercy Housing responded to their desire to address housing needs in areas well beyond those initially served. It wasn't a strategic plan that made Mercy Housing a national provider of affordable housing. It was the slow expansion brought about through co-sponsors donating land, linkages with others in the affordable housing field, or responding to urgent needs that demanded action.

Numbers tell the story. In 1987, right after Sister Terese Tracy resigned to take up community leadership, the Mercy Housing staff numbered only 24 people with a portfolio of 310 dwelling units. By 2000, as new co-sponsors joined the ministry, it ballooned to 269 employees overseeing 2,036 units. By 2019, Mercy Housing owned 328 properties, including over 23,000 apartment homes, and had 1,593 employees. Patricia O'Roark gives a sense of how such growth happened. "We went where people said, 'Please come, there's need here,'"[11] So Mercy went.

The period of the 1990s was marked by larger deals, greater complexity, and multiplicity. Mercy Housing was influenced by "an aggressively entrepreneurial spirit" alive among the affordable housing providers of the time.[12] Hardly any deal was a bad deal. What was not given as much attention was the infrastructure needed to handle the increased demand.

New co-sponsors also meant geographical spread. What was once a ministry within the geographical boundaries of the Omaha Regional Community now became one which reached from "sea to sea." One center could not handle it all. Mercy Housing needed regions. Apart from the founding region that became the Mercy Mountain Plains, it added Mercy California shortly after the Auburn and Burlingame Mercy Communities in California became co-sponsors.

Mercy Housing Northwest grew from the collaboration between Mercy Housing and Intercommunity Housing, an effort of multiple religious communities serving in the Northwest, some of which became co-sponsors of Mercy Housing. As Mercy Housing moved into Chicago, it built upon the foundation of what the Chicago Mercy Community had built in Milwaukee with Catherine's residence but soon expanded through its acquisition of Lakefront Supportive Housing. The growth required the creation of another region, Mercy Housing Lakefront.

The youngest of Mercy Housing's regions is Mercy Housing Southeast. In 1995, the Baltimore and North Carolina Regional Communities were partners in forming Mercy Housing Southeast. The two communities saw it as a way to implement programs and services related to their mission to address the unserved and underserved needs of people. Such small beginnings might not have required the creation of a new region, but those initial properties were soon expanded through another co-sponsoring community, the Sisters of Bon Secour. The Bon Secour sisters lent financial support to such projects as Mulberry Court in Greenville, South Carolina, at a time when the combination of hurricane conditions and delays threatened its future due to escalating costs for both construction and insurance.

Much expansion came through co-sponsors, but it also came as the result of groups seeking to partner with the organization. Before any of its founding sponsors became Mercy Housing co-sponsors, Intercommunity Housing in the Northwest sought out such a relationship. Prompted by the exhortation of the Leadership Conference of Women Religious to pursue collaboration among religious congregations, five communities working in the Northwest came together to see how they might work together to address common concerns.

According to Sister Charlotte Davenport CSP, all five religious communities — Sisters of St. Joseph of Peace, Sisters of

Providence, Dominican Sisters of Tacoma, and Dominican Sisters of Edmonds, joined in 1995 by the Sisters of the Holy Names of Jesus and Mary — were committed to reducing the number of children that were in situations that rendered them "at-risk" especially in the early years of life. Recognizing that children need stability during the first five years of life, the communities partnered to create more affordable family housing. In its founding document, we find these words that describe their journey together as they became Intercommunity Housing:

> A journey once taken alone
> we now choose to take together.
> Moving forward as Intercommunity Housing
> into a future filled with possibility,
> we walk without maps, but we walk confidently,
> and we walk with those who are homeless
> because we have chosen to be lights
> for each other, while on the way.

The undertaking was not without its challenges. In sharing the task, questions arose about whether there would be a loss of identity and charism, but Sister Charlotte Davenport reflects that rather than a loss of such vital elements, there was a strengthening. Nothing was deleted. She attributes that result to the fact that all the communities were rooted in the Gospel. In her words, "They were Vatican II congregations."[13]

The process was not easy, however. Like the early Mercy Housing pioneers, the sisters did not have a strong foundation in housing. Recognizing that they needed help from people with special expertise in housing, they hired a consultant to assist them in finding the best fit to bring their vision into reality. The consultant introduced them to the work of Mercy Housing.[14]

Sister Charlotte Davenport explains: "Mercy Housing was a natural fit. We were about the same goals and mission."[15] Mercy Housing shared their desire to provide stability for children through affordable family housing and, even more significant, had a model of supportive housing for the residents.

Initially two major properties were planned, one of 100 units and another of 150. Unfortunately, though they were identified and planned, the developer was unable to find the funding to go ahead. That is where becoming one with Mercy Housing made the difference. It helped to overcome the financing challenge and move the vision forward.

Unlike the Mercy sponsorship of Mercy Housing as a corporate ministry, the majority of Intercommunity's members could only commit their resources as provinces. The Sisters of St. Joseph of Peace were the only community at that time which could commit to full co-sponsors of Mercy Housing. Other founding communities of the Intercommunity Housing ministry contributed what resources they could but did not commit to co-sponsorship at that time. The region served by what became Mercy Housing Northwest grew beyond its small beginnings to serve communities in Washington, Oregon, and Idaho. As a result, today, over 5,000 families and seniors have affordable housing. In keeping with the founding sisters' vision, resident services focus on five key program areas: housing stability, health and wellness, community engagement, education, and financial well-being. Home becomes the hearth where children find the strength and stability to thrive in school and life.

Another housing agency, Lakefront Supportive Housing, followed the same pattern in Chicago. The organization shared common values with Mercy Housing. It was "committed to ending homelessness as a matter of social justice. Lakefront advocates for and provides quality permanent supportive housing for adults and families who are homeless or at risk of becoming homeless."[16] The organization focused upon managing supportive housing for unsheltered persons in the metropolitan Chicago area. In looking for partners to share the ministry, Lakefront Supportive Housing leaders came to the same conclusion that leaders of Intercommunity Housing had reached. Mercy Housing was a match to their mission and vision. Mark Angelini, President of Mercy Housing Lakefront, explains:

> Mercy Housing Lakefront has been around since 1986. It originally started as Lakefront SRO. SRO stood for single room occupancy. That was really a model that was focusing exclusively on the needs of chronically homeless individuals — individuals with a lot of mental health and addiction-related issues. About 2005, Mercy Housing came into the Chicago area, purchasing about 450 units of family housing in Austin on the west side. Lakefront SRO had gotten to a point where they really needed to merge in with a bigger partner. So, the entities merged and that's how we got Mercy Housing Lakefront.[17]

Mercy Housing Lakefront continues the commitment to supportive housing that is part of the legacy of the Chicago Mercy Community. A vital part of that legacy is St. Catherine's Residence in Milwaukee, which has served those in need of housing for over 125 years. In 2013, looking for a partnership that would ensure its continuing mission, the Board of Directors for St. Catherine's Residence entrusted its management and governance to Mercy Housing Lakefront. Preserving this vital ministry and its mission-based roots was the driving force in the transfer.[18] Over the next eight years, Mercy Housing Lakefront looked for a mission-driven partner who could carry this commitment into the future. In 2021, that partner became a reality as the ministry was entrusted to Hope House. As part of the transfer of St. Catherine's Residence to Hope House, Mercy Housing Lakefront provided capital needed for upcoming building maintenance, ensuring a smooth transition that further strengthens the property and provides residents with a high-quality environment in which to live.[19]

Lakefront Supportive Housing and Northwest Inter-Community Housing were not the only affordable housing ministries to see that joining Mercy Housing would be the best option for the people they served. Franciscan Ministries, a sponsored ministry of the Wheaton Franciscan Sisters, transferred 33 of their properties, encompassing 3,666 homes, to Mercy Housing in 2016. The transfer comprised almost 20% of Mercy's portfolio. This transfer expanded Mercy Housing's presence in Wisconsin, Arizona, Colorado, Iowa, Kentucky, and South Carolina.

Sister Pat Norton, Chair of the Sponsor Member Board for Wheaton Franciscan Healthcare, explained: "As the Sisters age and our numbers decrease, we wanted to transfer our corporate ministries while they are healthy, fiscally sound and have a strong sense of mission."[20] Susan Dillberg, President and CEO of Franciscan Ministries, echoed the same sentiments voiced by leaders of the other housing ministries which choose Mercy Housing to assume responsibility for their works. It was about resources and mission. In Dillberg's opinion, Mercy Housing had "an excellent reputation as a provider of quality affordable homes, and their mission aligns well with that of Franciscan Ministries; they are committed to serving communities with compassion and strongly believe in the power of affordable housing to enrich lives."[21]

Like all the various co-sponsoring religious communities and affordable housing agencies that became part of Mercy Housing, the creation of affordable housing units was not an end itself. It was a means through which people could attain the stability, safety, and support which would enable them to live with dignity and hope. Writing in support of Perfection Place, a Mercy Housing Southeast proposal for senior housing, Sister Rosalind Picot, then President of the Mercy Belmont community, wrote: "We do this because we believe in the right of all people to have certain basic rights, food, shelter, clothing, as well as other needs."[22] It was always about people.

One of the unifying themes that animated the work of the various ministries trying to address the needs of the under-sheltered or unsheltered was the connection between housing and health. The physical effects of being unsheltered are significant. Emergency rooms knew them all too well. In addition, the mental health toll paid by the unsheltered often results in depression, drug addiction, and domestic violence. As a former hospital administrator, none of this was lost on Sister Lillian. In 2005, she wrote:

> During my years as a hospital administrator, I became familiar with the impact that poverty and poor-quality housing tend to have on a person's health. I learned that chronic health concerns such as asthma, heart disease, and diabetes are all tied to the root problem of substandard housing, not to mention lead poisoning. I saw that the emergency room was often filled with people who were living in unhealthy conditions and suffering from malnutrition and preventable communicable diseases. Mentally ill patients with limited incomes had trouble sustaining housing

they could afford—a fact that often contributed to their mental instability. People trying to get by on low incomes were forced to spend most of their resources on housing—no matter how inadequate it might have been—instead of paying for critical follow-up care and prescriptions. It became clear to me that healthcare institutions had the capacity, the position of leadership in their communities, and the compassion to make an impact on housing in those communities.[23]

The reality that, without safe and stable housing, all persons are more susceptible to health issues such as chronic illnesses, weather-related health episodes, infections from inadequate sanitation access in their environments, as well as the inability to even afford the medicines needed to treat their illnesses, prompted Sister Lillian to find a way where the ministries of healthcare and housing could collaborate.[24]

As hospitals assessed community health needs, the challenge of adequate housing was always among the top factors needing to be addressed. It is not surprising that the combination of need, relationships, and complementary ministries would lead to collaboration. Two examples typical of such collaborations are those between Mercy Housing and St. Joseph's Hospital in Arizona, and another which brought together St. John's Hospital in Oxnard, California, with Mercy Housing.

In 1993, St. Joseph's Hospital offered Mercy Housing $1 million to start an office in Arizona to help alleviate the housing shortages. It was not hard for Sister Lillian and the Mercy Housing Board to accept such an attractive offer. Sometimes collaborations were a little more complex. In the mid-'90s, Jack

Burgis, Chief Financial Officer for Catholic Healthcare West, heard that St. John's Hospital in Oxnard had just acquired a recently closed hospital in the town. He convinced CHW to sell it and an adjoining parcel of land on generous terms to Mercy Housing for the development of homes for low-income families. The results were two projects: one, Casa Merced, for senior housing, and one for families, Casa San Juan. The endeavor not only supplied needed housing opportunities but also won political support for further developments.[25]

Such collaborations were ones of mutual gain. Mercy Housing was able to find significant support from the hospitals that generously provided office space, bridge loans, support for resident services and land, as well as potential board members and advocates for the ministry. The hospitals, on the other hand, received a pathway to addressing the health needs of the communities, great publicity, and often reduced numbers of unsheltered persons coming to emergency rooms. Each new health system that reached out to Mercy Housing (or vice versa) expanded the range of Mercy Housing's presence.

In 1999, recognizing the potential of such partnerships, Mercy Housing joined with seven Catholic healthcare systems to form the Strategic Health Care Partnership. The systems included Ascension Health, Bon Secours Health System, Catholic Health East, Catholic Health Initiatives, Catholic Healthcare Partners, Catholic Healthcare West, and St. Joseph Health System. Within five years of its establishment, approximately $325 million dollars funded the development of 54 properties in cities served by SHCP hospitals across the nation.[26] At the time Strategic Healthcare Partners started, Mercy housing had developed 5,300 units of affordable housing serving about 10,000 people. By 2003, through the alliances with their strategic partners, Mercy Housing had grown to 14,000 units serving over 40,000 people. The power of collaboration was palpable.

Brook Oaks Senior Residence in Waco, Texas, is a good example of what could happen when housing and healthcare joined together. Hospital facilities often have a limited lifespan. Such was the case for Providence Health Center's original facility in Waco, built almost 100 years before. When a new hospital replaced it in the southern part of the town, it was converted to a long-term care facility. Just four years later, in 2003, its next-door neighbor, St. Catherine's Center, a nursing home, had to be closed as well. Kent Keahey, then president of Providence Health Center, turned to Mercy Housing with the idea of converting the old hospital site into affordable housing to serve the large population of low-income seniors in Waco. Providence demolished the hospital, cleaned the site, and donated the seven-acre site to Mercy Housing in order to provide 55 units of affordable housing for low-income seniors.

Like other endeavors, it took more than the gift of land to make this a reality. The project was funded with a HUD 202 capital grant, HOME funds from the City of Waco, a private grant from the Cooper Foundation in Waco, and Affordable Housing Program funds from the Federal Home Loan Bank of Dallas. Understanding the health needs of the seniors and the importance of neighborhood revitalization, the apartments are designed for safety and residents' needs, and feature on-site supportive services and a healing garden.[27]

Recognizing the need to be close to the property for adequate rendering of services, Mercy Housing followed the same procedure used in turning over St. Catherine's in Milwaukee to an agency with a common mission. Today, Brook Oaks Senior Residence is operated by National Church Residences.

Mulberry Court in Greenville, North Carolina, is another good example. With the support of St. Francis Xavier Hospital leadership, Mercy Housing has become a member of the Greenville Catholic Collaboration, which unites hospital and housing staff with representatives from Catholic Charities member organizations in order to plan together how the needs of the community might best be addressed. St Francis' Community Affairs Department has arranged for a variety of health-enhancing services to be brought directly to Mulberry Court, a Mercy Southeast property, providing a dental van, monthly health screening services, classes in healthy cooking, and a specialized resource area in the Community Room that provides information, resource referrals, and handouts on healthy lifestyles. The significance of such efforts is seen in the city of Greenville's willingness to invest $800,000 for area environmental improvements such as sidewalks, street lighting, and landscaping.[28]

Not all the collaborations between SHCP and Mercy Housing were about bricks and mortar. Some were about systems, practices, and visioning. This was the case in the work with Franciscan Home Development, a developer of affordable housing in Cincinnati, sponsored by Catholic Health Partners. The area where its units were located was hit by civil unrest that resulted in plummeting occupancy rates. Many of the units were also experiencing maintenance problems predictable in 100-year-old buildings.

Jim Gravel and Jim Makos of CHP sat down with Stan Keisling of Mercy Housing to map out a strategy that would ensure the viability of the ministry going forward. Together they worked on an evaluation of operations, management systems, staff training, and turn-around strategies. All of this was rooted in mission, for Jim understood well that it takes more than good intentions to do good work. It takes leadership, an understanding of mission, financial, and business strategies, public relations expertise, and political will to get things done. As Jim put it: "You need to be cognizant of these things ... If you don't handle the business of doing good work, you won't be in the business of doing good work."[29]

What was accomplished through the Strategic Healthcare Partnership was significant. You might even say "massive." With new access to monies and opportunities throughout the United States, Mercy Housing was able to grow and expand its services.

The impact of such expansion brought life-enhancing external change in the circumstances for those in need of affordable housing, but it also brought change to Mercy Housing itself. No expansion was as impactful or brought more change than the coming together of Mercy Housing and the housing ministry of Catholic Charities, San Francisco.

For Your Reflection and Conversation

- The growth of Mercy Housing was marked by a culture of collaboration which brought together people and communities with a common mission. Today as Mercy Housing moves into the future, what norms do you believe should govern future collaborations?

- Each new collaboration or partnership changes an organization. Which merger or collaboration do you think was the most significant in making Mercy Housing what it is today?

CHAPTER 6

THE CALIFORNIA EXPERIENCE

On October 3, 2024, viewers of the national CBS Evening News were presented with startling data. In a segment on the homeless crisis in Los Angeles, reporter Adam Yamaguchi reported that LA had over 45,000 unsheltered individuals in a state that is home to almost 50% of the nation's unsheltered persons. To put it in perspective, the unsheltered population in Los Angeles is larger than any of the 600 U.S. towns identified in a 2018 survey as between 40,000 and 50,000. For persons working in the field of affordable housing, this was not news. It is a reality they have faced since the housing crisis of the 1980s.

California was once the land of promise and prosperity. In the Gold Rush era, people flocked to the new state seeking wealth and a new beginning. For many, it was a hard lesson in economics. Gold didn't flow in the streets and it took hard labor to pry it from the earth. Sacramento, now the capital of the state, had early squatters' riots because housing was limited and land prices were inflated by speculators. It was a cycle repeated over the course of the next hundred years.

Like many of the pioneer miners, desperate men and women

came to California during the Great Depression seeking relief from the Dust Bowl. They also faced tough times. Outside some California cities, tent cities called Hoovervilles emerged. The Hoovervilles were not unlike the encampments found in California's cities today.

World War II ushered in a post-war period of prosperity lasting from 1950 to 1970. Then things changed and California, along with the rest of the nation, went into what economists call the great "U-Turn." The economy transitioned from manufacturing to service industries where wages were lower. Almost 75% of the jobs generated in the 1980s were minimum wage jobs. The booming defense-related industries shrank, with 20,000 defense-related jobs lost in Southern California alone. Even the motion picture industry shrank in the early '80s.[1]

It wasn't just the loss of employment or low salaries that made housing an issue in California. It was the interplay among four dynamics: declining personal incomes, lack of affordable housing options, deep cuts in welfare programs, and an increasing number of persons facing personal issues that left them at high risk of homelessness.[2] The cuts in welfare programs and changes in mental health policy that released patients from state mental institutions to obtain care in community mental health centers resulted in many being lost through the cracks. Adding to the problem were the unsheltered Vietnam veterans suffering from PTSD and large numbers of individuals damaged by their addiction to mind-altering drugs such as crack cocaine or methamphetamines.

California was especially hard hit by these issues. Between 1950 and 1970, the population of California's mental asylums fell from 500,000 to 100,000. Many patients from state institutions returned to communities ill-prepared to support them.

Those without the stability and emotional support needed for employment found themselves on the streets. The intent of deinstitutionalizing mental healthcare was to provide a more humane and supportive mode of care, but a lack of resources and the scarcity of mental health clinics and family support left its promise unfulfilled.[3]

Cuts in welfare rolls were another key factor in the expansion of homelessness. Nationally, federal programs for persons experiencing poverty were reduced by $57 billion between 1982 and 1985. Additionally, some states also cut the General Assistance aid in half or didn't have a General Assistance program. Adding all this together, you have a predictable crisis. Decline in personal incomes, unaffordable housing, and increased rate of personal vulnerability created a broad class of precariously housed families and individuals who were only a paycheck away from eviction, or who had to make choices between food and rent or medicine and housing.[4] That was the state of things as Sister Lillian Murphy started her housing ministry in San Francisco. Little did she expect that the California region would come to comprise almost 50% of Mercy Housing's holdings and become the largest of its five regions.

At the time of her first venture into affordable housing, Sister Lillian was a hospital administrator at St. Mary's Hospital in San Francisco. It was right at the beginning of the 1980s. Sister Lillian had a keen sense of the interconnectedness of health and housing. As a hospital administrator, she saw first-hand what happened to patients who lacked adequate or safe housing. The lack of affordable housing in the city exacerbated the problem. St. Mary's Hospital, later part of the Catholic Healthcare West hospital system, purchased the abandoned Southern Pacific Hospital on Baker Street. With the support of the hospital and assisted by the John Stewart company, Sister Lillian moved to have the former hospital transformed into Mercy Terrace, 158 units of affordable senior housing. The first resident moved into the residence in 1982.

The John Stewart/Sr. Lillian link was strong and significant. He was a mentor to Sr. Lillian as she started Mercy Terrace and over time both had significant influence on affordable housing development in San Francisco. John's mentoring Sr. Lillian would start her on a 30-year dedication to the housing ministry. Their collaboration on Mercy Family Plaza resulted in the first Low-income Tax Credit property in California. A partnership and friendship that was enduring, Stewart gave the keynote address at Sister Lillian's retirement celebration in Denver.

When she started, Sister Lillian did not have any experience in affordable housing, but she did have a passionate interest in the field. That interest was sparked and fueled by her friendship with Sister Terese Tracy, who shared the stories of Mercy Housing's activities with her at various board meetings they attended together. When Sister Terese retired from her position as CEO of Mercy Housing, she encouraged Sister Lillian to apply for the position. She did and became its new CEO in 1986. At the time, Mercy Housing's portfolio consisted of four properties in Idaho, one in Denver, and scattered-site housing in Kansas City and Omaha.

Sister Lillian wasted little time in expanding Mercy Housing's efforts in California. Knowing the critical need for housing in the Bay Area, Sister Lillian sent Sister Diane Clyne to establish an office there. Sister Diane describes it this way: "It was sort of a closet affair. It was a desk at the end of a hallway with no windows and no doors and no way to have privacy. We set up files and began to work immediately on the development at Mercy Family Plaza."[5]

While these early Mercy Housing initiatives in San Francisco were underway, something much bigger was happening behind the scenes, something that significantly impacted the future of Mercy Housing itself. It began in 1987 when Jack Burgis, the new CFO of Catholic Healthcare West, was captured by the vision of the Mercy Housing's ministry. Sister Lillian and Sarah Smith had just asked the CHW finance committee for $1 million only to be told it wouldn't happen. After the meeting, Jack met with Sister Lillian and told her: "This is not going to remain on my watch as a non-starter. It's going to become a real part of our mission if I have anything to say about it."[6] Sister Lillian quickly tapped him for the board of Mercy Housing. As CFO of Catholic Healthcare West, one of Jack's responsibilities was to sit on the board of St. Mary's Hospital, which owned the Old Southern Pacific property adjacent to the newly opened Mercy Terrace. Jack was successful in convincing the hospital to either give the land to Mercy Housing or sell it to them for very favorable terms. That collaboration between Mercy Housing and CHW allowed work on Mercy Housing's first California development, Mercy Family Plaza, to move forward.

Like the earlier Mercy Housing pioneers, Sister Diane says it was a "learn as you go" operation. What made it work was team-work. As the owner's representative, Sister Diane was responsible for overseeing the project. It was more than just the bricks and mortar aspects. It was working to build community relationships. Mercy Family Plaza was to be home to 36 families on a shared site with the seniors living at Mercy Terrace. The vision was to create an intergenerational community and Sister Diane worked with everyone involved to make that happen.

While Sister Lillian did the challenging work of finding fund-ing, Sister Diane had to make sure that the project stayed true to the guidelines laid down by funders and permitting agencies. There is always risk involved during the building process. A story shared by Sister Diane highlights that risk. The remaining buildings on the property were designated as historical properties, and historical preservation tax credits had been awarded for their renovation. When tax credits for historical preservation are granted, they are dependent upon nothing occurring to seriously damage the building. If that happens, the tax credit disappears. The work on the powerhouse at Mercy Family Plaza was concurrent with the huge Loma Prieta earthquake that hit San Francisco in 1989. Severe damage occurred throughout the city. Needless to say, it was with fear and trepidation that Sister Diane went to inspect the powerhouse and other buildings on the Baker Street property, knowing that damage from the quake could imperil funding. Fortunately, no major damage was done and the tax credits were safe. Had it been different, the whole project would have failed.[7]

The third San Francisco project was Notre Dame Plaza, another senior housing development directly across the street from Mission Dolores. It was different from Mercy Family Plaza in that it was a shared project with the housing division of Catholic Charities San Francisco and the Notre Dame Sisters. The property was the former high school of the Notre Dame Sisters, and their community treasurer was the owner representative but not the developer. Sister Diane's challenge with this endeavor was to bring all the participants to a unified vision. For the sisters, seeing a cherished high school and convent transformed into something entirely new was both satisfying and painful. Buildings carry sacred memories, so sensitivity is vital. The beauty and sensitivity of the final result was something all the entities involved could own with pride. Jane Graf considers the outcome as "an example of what communities can do together."[8]

An essential element needed by all affordable housing developers is a reputation built on keeping promises, achieving results, and persevering efforts in the face of challenges. The first three Mercy Housing developments in San Francisco did just that for the Bay Area. The successes primed lenders and civic leaders to be more receptive to future proposals. The Bay area is not Sacramento, however, and what works successfully in San Francisco does not always work well in Sacramento. Separated by 90 miles, the two communities were vastly different in needs, civic cultures, and opportunities. What they did have in common was the urgent need for more affordable housing both for families and for seniors.

The story of Mercy Housing in Sacramento began in 1989 when the Sisters of Mercy of Burlingame and of Auburn both became Mercy Housing Founding communities by entering into a relationship of co-sponsorship. The two communities had been approached by Sister Lillian Murphy, who believed that more could be achieved by expanding through collaboration. Both the Burlingame and Auburn communities were eager to address housing issues in their local areas. An office of Mercy Housing was already functioning in San Francisco but needed someone to take the lead in Sacramento. It found that housing champion in Sister Mary Monica Burns.

Sister Mary Monica was part of the Auburn leadership team that made the decision to co-sponsor Mercy Housing. At the conclusion of Sister Mary Monica's term on the leadership team, she went to Denver to be trained as a developer and then returned to Sacramento to start her work. Like other Mercy sisters investing their talents in Mercy Housing, Sister Mary Monica had little if any prior experience with housing but she was very skilled in working with people.

Jane Graf describes Sister Mary Monica this way:

She was fearless, a force. When she started working on St. Francis Terrace, she had street smarts and really worked at making transactions happen. Nothing was impossible to her. She made herself vulnerable. Everybody who worked with Monica loved her … Every moment was busy, no task too inconsequential. She would go on every site visit. She became a construction expert, always helpful. There was nothing she couldn't do.[9]

Sister Mary Monica needed all that energy and determination for the work ahead.

In her role as developer, Sister Monica had partnered with the Chamber of Commerce's housing division to determine that affordable housing was the biggest perceived need in the city. The project, however, did not get off to a promising start. The land on which St. Francis Terrace would be built was donated to Mercy Housing by the Diocese of Sacramento. Unfortunately, no prior work with the adjoining school community or the neighborhood had taken place before the diocese told the parish about its plan for the land. Neighborhood and parish community resistance was fast and powerful. This was where Sister Mary Monica's years as an administrator and her natural relational skills came to the fore.

A mediator was hired to bring people together: two from each of the various perspectives. Sr. Monica's creativity in solving testy questions was greatly needed. One such challenge was moving a historically preserved house down several streets to a new site when the streets were not wide and were tree-laden. Her willingness to adjust designs to meet neighbors' desires resulted in a facility that won praise for its architectural impact as well as for the services to the families who call it home. The success of St. Francis Terrace smoothed the way for her next undertaking, the building of Russell Manor, a 65-unit senior housing residence in "housing poor" South Sacramento.

Jack Burgis's impact on the growth of Mercy Housing in California did not stop with its initial projects. In 1991, Jack was on the board of Catholic Charities, San Francisco. He was present when Frank Hudson shared that Archbishop John Quinn was nervous about two properties which Catholic Charities Housing planned to develop using tax credits. Specifically, he was worried about the exposure that the archdiocese might incur if they proceeded with the plan. It was at that point that Jack approached Frank, saying: "I think I've got a deal for you. I think that Mercy Housing ought to take this over and run with it because I think they're prepared to take the risk and have the expertise or are developing the expertise to really become the major player in affordable housing."[10] It sounded like a win-win but it was challenging to break down the reluctance of some board members to turn over their rather sizable portfolio. Jane Graf remembers the moment as one of convergence. "Charities wanted to move this housing work into an organization that shared their ethos and drive at a time when Sister Lillian, through Mercy Housing, wanted to expand into California. It was a natural coming together."[11]

The merger of Mercy Housing and the housing division of Catholic Charities, San Francisco, brought more than properties to Mercy Housing. It brought Jane Graf and her staff into the Mercy Housing family. Jane, chosen to head up Mercy Charities Housing, identifies two significant aspects that Mercy Housing gained through the merger:

1. Catholic Charities housing brought a staff that had extensive experience and education in housing. It was not a "learn as you go" operation.

2. It held a housing portfolio of over 20 properties, more than doubling Mercy Housing's holdings.

On the other hand, those joining the organization from Catholic Charities Housing found:

1. A culture that was comfortable with risk taking and had the resources to get things done

2. Greater autonomy and freedom to act and, especially for women, to lead

3. A directed mission focus[12]

The merger with Catholic Charities Housing was not the only merger that created what is now Mercy Housing California. The Santa Cruz Community Development Corporation had about 14 to 15 properties which were fiscally distressed. Mercy Housing worked with them to transfer their properties to Mercy Housing. That same support and assistance was given to other smaller organizations which sought help. What was not small, however, was the coming together of Mercy Charities Housing and the acquisition of Rural California Housing Corporation (RCHC), which was a major agency in the Sacramento region and the rural areas of California, in particular. Jack Burgis notes that the merger, happening in 2000, brought with it a model of housing that was new ground for Mercy Housing, that of self-help housing.[13]

Stan Keisling, who served as CEO of RCHC for almost 14 years, explains: "The difference between self-help and habitat is that you're building a neighborhood at a time. The families are the builders and neighbors for each other — they build a community, build 8 or 10 houses at a time. And really build a place where people stay for a very long time. That was the primary function of RCHC when I joined."[14]

Since its inception in 1967, RCHC expanded access to quality affordable housing for Californians living in rural counties in the northern part of California. From equipping low-income families with the financing and know-how to build their own homes to developing service-enriched rental housing, RCHC has developed 3,200 single-family homes and more than 1,000 rental apartments.[15] Founded out of Woodland, California, it had a strong Yolo County emphasis but extended beyond that county to encompass a 14-county service area. Many of the projects developed by RCHC were along the I-80 Corridor, linking the two Mercy Housing offices of San Francisco and Sacramento. The coming together of the two groups created Mercy Housing California, the second largest developer of affordable housing in California. Together they had 43 years of experience, employed more than 365 people, and served some 23,000 low-income persons.[16]

The importance and urgency of the work done by RCHC is captured in a report by the Housing Assistance Council, which pointed out that:

> The 2010 Census revealed that of the approximately 116 million occupied housing units available in the United States, 25 million units are located in rural and small communities. Over 5 percent, or 1.5 million, of these homes are considered either moderately or severely substandard. For example, more than 30 percent of the nation's housing units lacking hot and cold piped water are in rural and small-town communities, and on some Native American lands

the incidence of homes lacking basic plumbing is more than 10 times the national level.[17]

Rural housing was a critical need in agricultural California. Frequently rural areas lacked the needed infrastructure to build housing, things like water and sewage systems. Farm workers were particularly at risk of being unsheltered. Sister Maria Padilla, a member of the Auburn community, had long brought this need to light.

She grew up in a farmworker family and knew first-hand the hardships it involved. In her ministry to farm workers, she found that housing provided by growers came at a cost. She was sometimes refused access to the families who lived in migrant housing by the owners. Such a refusal meant folks who had no transportation could not have Mass celebrated in the camp or have their children receive religious formation. Workers who protested against unsafe or dilapidated housing risked losing the housing provided. Given the sponsors' priorities, the merger with Rural California Housing Corporation brought new opportunities to address the pressing needs of the workers.

As RCHC developed a reputation for thoughtful rural development, its leaders took pains to share their expertise and access to funding with smaller grassroots groups. They knew they couldn't do it all and were committed to collaborations. "Many nascent community organizations knew exactly what kind of housing their community needed and had great ideas for developing it, but state and federal agencies couldn't take the risk of funding them,"[18] said Greg Sparks, former Deputy Director of RCHC and former Vice President of Mercy Housing California. RCHC used its credibility and reputation to leverage funding and acquire sites that were beyond the ability of its smaller partners to acquire.

"Other developers might balk at the practice of helping other groups build capacity, add homes to their portfolio, and eventually create more competition for deals, but that wasn't RCHC's thinking. We wanted as many organizations developing quality rural housing as possible,"[19] said Sparks. Along the way, RCHC discovered that doing sweat equity[20] single-family housing was insufficient to meet the needs of the unsheltered. It was at that point that they began to expand beyond that housing model. In the early 1990s, they partnered as co-developers on two Sacramento communities, Quinn Cottages and Saint Francis Terrace. It was after that experience that MHC and RCHC made the momentous decision to merge organizations in 2000. It was a mutually beneficial coming together of two housing providers. Stephen Daues, former Regional Director of Real Estate Development for Mercy Housing California in Sacramento, reflects:

> Merging these two organizations has meant the best of both worlds … We have expansive national and statewide resources in terms of capital and political relationships, and yet I get to work like a grassroots community developer. We take on hard, complex developments and do them well because we really are local and carry the scrappy RCHC rural experience with us.[21]

The merger brought new energies and focus to Mercy Housing, complementing what was already in place. The collaboration around Quinn Cottages provided a model of how serving the formerly homeless could look. The self-help properties built lasting communities, using a different model than Mercy Housing used in urban centers. The merger also brought increased volume in the California market. To the work of RCHC, it brought a national lens. It significantly increased capital, allowing more risk, and strengthened its ability to continue a rural experience. It also responded to the profound desire of Mercy Housing sponsors to respond to the needs of families whose children were often at risk because of lack of housing.

While all that sounds wonderful, it did not happen without a struggle. Although key leaders like Jane Graf and Stan Kiesling were friends and collaborators, buy-in had to permeate the whole team. RCHC had just ended earlier merger negotiations with another regional non-profit, and the staff was first told about renewed merger talks with Mercy Housing at a staff retreat. Stan describes the reaction as: "Unbelievably bad, unbelievably bad. It wiped out the entire good feelings that people had had for the previous two days."[22]

Stephen Daues, at the time an assistant project manager, attributes the response to fears around the new management company that RCHC had just started. Staff feared a merger would bring about cost-cutting efficiencies that would be achieved by cutting back on the fledgling management company. Change always raises fear. Merger talks were put on hold for another six months. Looking back, Jane Graf shares that: "It was probably the best thing that could have ever happened because it allowed for us to have, I guess, for lack of a better way to describe it, a little courtship between the organizations."[23]

It was a learning moment, setting the pattern for future merger conversations. Those conversations would be much more deliberate. Jane points out that trust had to be built, not only between leaders, but throughout the organizations by bringing functional groups together … service people with service people, developers with developers. Cross-functional groups were then brought together. It all took time, but it paid off.[24] For both organizations, the merger was not about business so much as it was about mission. Jane Graf reflects that it seems that no ego was involved, especially between leaders at the highest level. People were focused on making sure that the merger made sense because everyone wanted to keep doing the good work that was being done. "Once people figured out that this, in fact, made sense, from that perspective, they were right on."[25]

In addition to an expansion of services, the creation of Mercy Housing California extended the footprint of the ministry throughout the whole region of the Sisters of Mercy Auburn Regional Community presence. Both urban and rural areas were found in the Mercy Housing portfolio. The importance of the merger was highlighted by Jane Graf as she looked back in 2022. "In my years with Mercy, I think it was by far the most important move in California, and this happened in 2000. It was just an incredible opportunity and benefit and the best thing that could have ever happened. I know there are other mergers that we'll contemplate in the future, but it's hard to imagine one that will create the kind of results that this merger created."[26]

It wasn't only mergers that created growth in the California market. It was also the partnership between Mercy Housing and Catholic Healthcare West. From the beginning of the ministry in California, Catholic Healthcare West, the healthcare system founded by Sisters of Mercy of Auburn and Burlingame, supported and helped finance Mercy Housing's efforts. The partnership between the two set the pattern of what would later develop into Strategic Healthcare Partnership. While earlier healthcare support often came in the form of free office space or support for those in the ministry, CHW started the partnership with land donations, bridge loans, or reduced-cost sales of property. Mercy Terrace led the way but was soon followed by other surplus land donations. It was this dynamic that led Mercy Housing to address needs in the Southern California area.

Sister Amy Bayley, a member of the Burlingame Mercy community, arrived at Mercy Housing's San Francisco office in 1995. Shortly after, she was assigned to develop Mercy Housing's outreach in Southern California. Initially, she worked out of the San Francisco office. In Sister Amy's words: "It was a difference of distance and number of airplane rides."[27] The first of the Southern California properties was in Oxnard. It was a senior housing property located on the site of the former Swift Lying-In Hospital. True to the practice of involving neighbors in the planning process, developers for Mercy Housing listened to the surrounding community. They discovered there was resistance to the idea of demolishing the old hospital with its mission style. Listening to community, it was decided to revise plans and to renovate the Spanish-colonial style building. A larger structure was built behind it with the same white stucco walls and red tile roof. The option allowed Mercy Housing to build 40 units of affordable housing for seniors. Dara Kovel, project manager, noted that although the cost was more than building a brand-new building, the renovation preserved the nature of the neighborhood and eased tensions with homeowners of the historical district.[28]

Oxnard was not the only Southern California location to see Mercy Housing activity. Bakersfield was also such an area. With the support of Jim Burke, a local businessman, and under the auspices of Mercy Hospital, land was acquired for affordable housing development in the southeastern part of the city. It was a profoundly underserved community both in terms of infrastructure and social services. The new housing complex would be home to 50 families. When the residents of the area heard about the project, they were ready to resist the proposal.

Sister Amy, an educator by training, set about exploring the root causes of the resistance. She discovered that their concerns were rooted in worries about what the additional 50 families would do to the neighborhood, which already lacked adequate fire and police services as well as adequate infrastructure. Recognizing that knowledge reduces fear, Sister Amy addressed their concerns, helping them understand the benefits brought to them through housing. The result was a significant lessening of community fears, but some nervousness still remained. Convinced that seeing is believing, Sister Amy asked Jim Burke to borrow his plane for a "field trip." Four leaders of the community were invited to tour Mercy Housing properties in the Bay Area. Jane Graf and Sister Amy took the representatives on a tour of the properties in San Francisco so they could see what was possible for themselves. They returned as strong advocates for the project!

The manner in which Sister Amy went about pre-development work differed from what might be called a "community developer" approach. In that approach, developers work to overcome opposition. It is not focused on an educational approach which seeks to win support by influencing vision and understanding. It is the latter model that became normative for Mercy Housing California. Work in San Diego and Los Angeles followed quickly and utilized that same model of predevelopment relationship building. Sometimes expansion of the work happened unexpectedly. Such was the case when, similar to the Diocese of San Francisco, the Diocese of Los Angeles transferred several housing properties from the Diocese of Los Angeles to Mercy Housing.

The Sisters of Mercy in California were not the only religious community that would be actively engaged with Mercy Housing in California. In 1997, two other communities became co-sponsors, the Sisters of St. Joseph of Orange and the Daughters of Charity, Province of the West. The increasing growth in Mercy Housing activity throughout Southern California demanded more presence than could be provided long range. Recognizing the need for an office in the south state, the St Joseph Healthcare System of the Sisters of St. Joseph of Orange provided a three-year grant of $300,000 per year to fund such an office. Dara Kovel, who worked with Sister Amy on the Oxnard property, was asked to open the new Mercy Housing office in Anaheim to serve the south state.

Through the Strategic Healthcare Partnership, of which St. Joseph Healthcare System is part, other properties have been developed. Among the properties are Linbrook Court and Casa Alegre in Anaheim, Buena Vista Senior Housing in Orange County, and a collaboration with Mission Hospital in San Juan Capistrano, which is focused on family housing. Maya Dunne, Assistant Vice President of Foundation and Community Outreach for the St. Joseph Health System, comments:

> The Housing plight of the nation is staggering. The Strategic Healthcare Partnership has meant that we as healthcare providers have had a much greater impact than we could as one health system. It is rewarding to know that each family and person who has been blessed to now have a safe and affordable place to call home will be healthier as a result of our working together.[29]

Plans for Mercy Housing to renovate the former Motherhouse of the Sisters of Joseph into senior housing started shortly before a change in California state law passed in 2023. The Affordable Housing on Faith Lands Act makes it easier for faith communities to use their land for the development of affordable housing. The new law would have been able to be applied to the Villa St. Joseph development, helping to ease its transition into senior housing. The law, a welcome boon to affordable housing advocates, streamlines the approval processes needed to move forward the project. For those working to provide more affordable housing, the law provides a powerful new tool. Doug Shoemaker, then President of Mercy Housing California, shared: "We're looking forward to partnering with more congregations who are ready to turn underused land into high-quality affordable homes.[30] Sister Diane Hejna CSJ sums up the delight of the sisters as they handed over their home to their neighbors:

> As Sisters of St. Joseph, we are called to reach out to serve the dear neighbor. We are welcoming of those in need today. Our renovated Motherhouse will offer a warm welcome, hospitality, and a home for seniors. It is our hope that, thanks to this thoughtful policy, more congregations will have the opportunity to follow suit and create welcoming affordable housing on the lands they own.[31]

Villa St. Joseph was not the only collaboration between the Sisters of St. Joseph and Mercy Housing. The Daughters of Charity, Province of the West, joined in the efforts of Mercy Housing California's outreach into Southern California when they joined as co-sponsors in 1997. As a sponsor, the Daughters of Charity asked Mercy Housing to look at the feasibility of using their 20-acre site in downtown Santa Barbara for an affordable housing development for families. It was land that the Daughters of Charity had owned since the 1850s. Mercy Housing immediately began an extensive community advisory process that reached out to multiple groups, neighbors, environmental groups, and city and country officials — everyone who had a stake in the future of the area. One of the aspects of the conversation involved being faithful to the Mission Revival architectural style that was characteristic of Santa Barbara. The efforts paid off. David Gustafson, then City of Santa Barbara Community Development Director, commented: "Mercy Housing California earned the faith and trust of the city through a community outreach program beyond any I have experienced."[32]

This was not a quick process. Sister Amy points out that it was really a 10-year process, starting in 1997. "It included many, many elements of developments, entitlements, and annexations and Fish and Game coming in because there's streams through the site. But the good news was that the entire community supported it."[33] The end result was St. Vincent's Gardens with 75 affordable apartment homes for families and individuals, and Villa Caridad which has 95 affordable apartment homes for seniors. The two residences were dedicated in 2009.

The impact of Mercy Housing on California's affordable housing scene was illustrated in a housing dashboard created in 2021. The dashboard reported that Mercy Housing California's portfolio contained:

     Properties owned   151
     Units owned   10,389
     81% of properties were providing services
     52% of the properties were family properties
     32% of the properties were senior properties
     16% of the properties were supportive properties
     14 developments were in construction while
     another 21 were under development
     Total units in process were 3,703

The story of Mercy Housing California mirrors the experiences of Mercy Housing ministry throughout its history. It was planted and nurtured by sisters like Sisters Monica Burns, Amy Bayley, and Patsy Harney, who left satisfying ministries to meet the critical needs of the unsheltered. The presence of the sisters witnessed the community's dedication to housing and, like the first seven pioneer sisters of Mercy Housing, they had learned from their experiences.

The merger with Catholic Charities Housing San Francisco and that with Rural California Housing Corporation brought newness to the overall organization. From Catholic Charities Housing, San Francisco, Mercy Housing gained trained and dedicated housing developers and managers. That transfusion of trained professionals permeated out into the whole of Mercy Housing. From Rural California Housing Corporation, it gained experience with a diversity of housing options. Just the size of Mercy Housing California alone made new lines of credit and funding available to all of Mercy Housing.

Perhaps the last gift that Mercy Housing California brought to the whole of Mercy Housing was its spirit of flexibility and innovation. The wide diversity of the state, the multiplicity of its needs, and the staunch support it elicited from civic leaders, banks, and corporations, all created opportunities to experiment with new ways to deliver services. The challenge to address special needs such as housing for persons with HIV, Veterans Housing Communities, or housing for those in the LGBTQ community required that flexibility of approach. It was challenging and complicated. Responding not only demanded vision and commitment; it required the creativity and collaboration of persons skilled in affordable housing development. That is the next chapter of the story.

For Your Reflection and Conversation

- Mercy Housing California's portfolio of properties comprises almost 50% of Mercy Housing's holdings. Given its size and the diversity of its holdings, what do you feel is its impact on the whole of Mercy Housing? What are the particular gifts offered to the whole by other regions?

- Prior to its merger with Catholic Charities Housing, San Francisco, many Mercy Housing leaders were people who had learned on the job. With the merger, it had an infusion of trained professional affordable housing personnel. What kinds of culture changes do you think would emerge in such a change? What culture changes have emerged during your own association with Mercy Housing?

CHAPTER 7

FROM CONCEPT TO COMPLETION, THE WORK OF DEVELOPMENT

Statistics showing that Mercy Housing has helped provide over 100,000 homes impacting a quarter million people are impressive.[1] What is even more impressive is how much work went into that achievement. That is the work of Mercy Housing's developers, who move the concept to reality. To anyone not in the affordable housing field, seeing a new housing project being built is about contractors, bankers, and architects. Little is known about what the Urban Land Institute calls "Ten Principles for Developing Affordable Housing." The principles urge developers to:

Inspire Leadership
Build Community Support and Trust
Learn the Alphabet . . . and Do the Math
Know Your Market and Your Customers
Nurture Partnership
Select Sites for Opportunity and Choice
Strive for Healthy, Balanced Communities
Use Design to Foster Community, Safety, and Pride

Empower the Residents
Orchestrate Sustainability[2]

Translating those principles into action is a formidable task, but that is what Mercy Housing developers do every day.

Dara Kovel, a Mercy Housing California developer in the early 2000s, uses the metaphor of a symphony conductor to describe the task. According to Kovel, the conductor has to keep all the pieces together and move forward. In her words: "Someone has to do that."[3] Another metaphor might be the puzzle-maker. There are so many details, big and little, which must be fitted together to move the concept to completion, and many things can pop up along the way to complicate or even bring about the failure of a proposed development. The possibility of such a failure is so real that Steven Spears, former CFO of Mercy Housing, notes that there was a line item in the budget called "dead deal."[4]

In reviewing the Urban Land Institute's ten principles, all resonate with the way in which Mercy Housing goes about development. From its inception, there has been dynamic leadership of the ministry. Its first Presidents came to the ministry with an abundance of administrative experience, a passion for the ministry, and the ability to build collaborative teams. Such qualities compensated for their initial lack of experience in affordable housing because they not only knew where to find competent assistance, they were quick to use such resources. An essential quality possessed by leaders at all levels of the organization was the ability to help others see what could be done, to draw others into that vision, and then to deliver the goods. As the Urban Land Institute points out:

> People leading the effort to develop affordable housing
> will see the problem, dream of something better,

and exhibit the passion and persistence needed to overcome barriers and achieve results. And they must inspire elected officials and community advocates to help lead the effort.[5]

That is exactly what the leaders of Mercy Housing have done from the beginning. As Patricia O'Roark first declared: "We can do better."

While visionary leadership is necessary, so was practicality. Not every opportunity was in the best interests of the ministry. Colin Morgan-Cross, Vice President for Real Estate Development in Mercy Housing Northwest, points out that developers must seriously explore the potential of each site in terms of access. It is not feasible to build in areas that lack such things as access to transportation, medical facilities, grocery stores, schools, or childcare opportunities — even if the property is donated land. The needs of families or seniors who live in the proposed property will not be met. Families can't thrive in food deserts. Parents can't hold down jobs that they can't reach due to a lack of transportation. For seniors as well as families, access to healthcare is necessary to avoid small illnesses ballooning into major ones.

One of the most important first steps taken by Mercy Housing developers is community assessment. Although affordable housing rises to the top of community assessments carried out by healthcare institutions across the country, there is no guarantee that the civic community supports the undertaking. That recognition gap can cause substantial delays. Dara Kovel describes that dynamic as she encountered it in Anaheim, California. The city lacked affordable housing options for the many service workers and hotel workers whose employment was connected to Disneyland. Whole families sometimes lived in hotel rooms or their cars. Unable to find housing they could afford, many workers endured long commutes. The need was compelling.

The Urban Land Institute puts it succinctly:

> Housing that is affordable to working families and close to their places of employment is a critical component of a region's economic health. Workers who must commute long distances because they cannot find affordable housing close to their jobs spend an excessive amount of time on the roadways that could be spent at work, and are thereby less productive and more frustrated.[6]

It quickly became apparent that, although the need was there, the civic will to provide affordable family housing was not. Whether caused by the dynamics of "not in my backyard," ethnic prejudice toward immigrant workers, or fear, the dynamic slowed the progress of development. The civic community had not grasped the economic benefits that affordable family housing could provide for the city. It simply wasn't clear to civic leadership. What is clear is that determination and perseverance on the part of Mercy Housing personnel caused efforts to move forward. Since a large family housing development was not initially possible, Kovel and her partners started with a 26-unit development focused on housing for those with HIV or AIDS. The success of that undertaking planted the seed for the next step, a senior housing complex. After five years, building on the success of the first two projects and the trust which had been built with the civic community, Mercy Housing's first family housing project in Anaheim started its construction in 2004.[7]

Transparency in the development stage of a project is a vital part of Mercy Housing's approach. An example of how successful such an approach can be is illustrated in the story of Savannah Gardens in Savannah, Georgia. This project was focused on an area of Savannah that had become a slum region. Housing, meant to be temporary, was built for workers during WWII. It was meant to be torn down after the war but instead remained, falling into disrepair. Owners of the housing units profited through their rents without maintaining the houses.

As Mercy Housing planned for the future, it brought together all the people impacted by the transformation of the area. Neighbors, residents, civic leaders, extended neighbors, and business leaders all had a seat at the table. What resulted was a 439-unit affordable housing development designed for community. Edna Jackson, former mayor of Savannah, shares: "We were a team. We worked together. We made decisions together."[8] Such collaboration ensures that residents feel heard and real needs are met. It builds a sense of ownership in the community itself.

For developers, there is another advantage to extensive consultation in the preliminary stages of the development. It reduces the chances for legal challenges to the project as well as reducing resistance to the development from neighborhoods, civic agencies or leaders, or businesses. It demands that developers not be just technicians skilled at constructing buildings. They must also be adept at reading a community's climate and readiness for projects to go forward.

Early Mercy Housing developers were eager to discover possibilities for new facilities. Energy was focused on growth and expansion. Sister Lillian Murphy once noted that Sister Geraldine Hoyler CSC provided a needed balance to her own focus on expansion by calling attention to long-term sustainability. "I had all these crazy ideas about what we should be doing and she [Geraldine] would have to go make them happen. And she'd say, "Well we could do this and this but we can't do this."[9] Sister Geraldine was all about the discipline needed to sustain what was being achieved. That issue was at the heart of what was called the "Transformation," which occurred from 2005 to 2008. During the process, 13 of Mercy Housing's 15 senior corporate officers would leave the organization.

The catalyst for the reorganization of Mercy Housing was provided in a study commissioned by Sister Lillian. She recruited Shekar Narasimhan of Beekman and Associates, an authority on the finance of multifamily and subsidized low-income housing, to assess the organization and financial structure, as well as Mercy Housing's operational systems. His findings, while greatly concerning, contained a path forward. He basically stated that the current structure and financial situation were unsustainable: "Beekman recommends transformational change."[10] Alexander Von Hoffman provides an in-depth evaluation of this Institutional change in the study, "The Transformation of Mercy Housing." He points out:

> In 2005, their leader and Chief Executive Officer, Sister Lillian Murphy, had precipitated fundamental change when her vision of enlarging operations to meet the growing needs of low-income Americans collided with a hemorrhaging balance sheet that threatened the existence of the company.[11]

Sister Lillian's ability to tap into the energies of communities of women religious, plus the support flowing from the Strategic Healthcare Partnership, had accelerated the pace and extent of Mercy Housing's undertakings. By the time of the Transformation, Mercy Housing was active in 18 states. By the end of the process three years later, holdings were focused on nine core markets. The causes precipitating the changes were multiple. As projects multiplied, so did long-term sustainability challenges such as cost of deferred maintenance, provision of support services, and unexpected emergencies caused by weather events. The types of development initiatives also played a part as well. Special needs housing, such as those for the chronically unsheltered or the mentally ill, demanded more resources and support — resources and support that were not always adequately budgeted in the yearly budgeting process.

In a sense, the Transformation of Mercy Housing was about making the math work while preserving the mission. Lack of analysis prior to acceptance of new developments, or of acceptance of older properties that needed extensive rehabilitation, caused cost overruns beyond what the ministry's resources could absorb. Von Hoffman illustrates the problem by referencing the purchase of a portfolio of troubled properties from ShoreBank in Chicago. The math was way off and ended up underestimating by half the actual cost for rehabilitation of the properties. Even smaller costs such as replacing an elevator sometimes exceeded the property's reserves.[12] Such miscalculations helped bring the whole ministry to the brink of financial disaster.

Trying to keep everything in balance was challenging for developers who were responsible for finding the funding to make developments work. By 2005, Mercy's property acquisitions had generated 57 separate property corporations: 14 property-holding corporations, 17 general partner corporations, 5 bond property corporations, and 38 limited liability corporations. Just in case that wasn't enough, Mercy entities were the general or co-general partners in 94 separate partnerships. Such a complex network of corporations, each unique, demanded revised ways of exercising oversight.[13]

One of the outcomes of the Transformation involved adjusting the structure to allow more responsibility to be held by local regional leadership.[14] Developers and regional leaders had to exercise fiscal discipline and transparency. Communication was critical. Relationships with partners had to keep them informed at each step of the way, whether the data was positive or negative. Such qualities allowed developers to approach bankers and funding agencies from a stance of trust. By creating strong collaborative relationships with funders, developers were more able to ask for waivers or extensions if major problems occurred. This was essential during the pandemic when construction delays due to supply chain issues were common.

While the organization itself was experiencing vast changes, the developers of Mercy Housing steadfastly continued their work. Not all their activity was visible. Much time was spent behind the scenes getting to know needs, the local environment, and market. With that knowledge, developers were more able to adapt to the unique needs of each community. A team approach, which included developers, construction leaders, architects, and representatives from property management, gave birth to innovation and creative problem solving. This is most evident in buildings that are considered historical preservation properties.

Taking on the revisioning of a historical landmark challenges the imagination, creativity, sensitivity, and skills of developers. In most cases the building set for renovation has fallen into disuse or, in a worst-case scenario, dereliction. Since funding sources often include historical preservation tax credits, a mishap which damages or destroys the external historical ambiance can mean loss of the whole deal. Located in downtown areas that lack land for new development, or in areas where whole neighborhoods need revitalization, renovation of historical buildings provides a path for meeting housing needs as well as neighborhood renewal. Community involvement is vital since the historical site carries community memory and meaning. One example of such an undertaking is Mercy Housing Southeast's Heritage Place and Heritage Corner & Row Apartments. Opening their doors in 2015, they stand on the grounds of two of Savannah's most storied buildings: Charity Hospital and the Florence Street School.

Savannah had a scarcity of safe, affordable housing, especially in the historic, predominantly African American Cuyler Brownville neighborhood. In the 1990s, the neighborhood had declined from its former glory and vitality. The city of Savannah was eager to renew the neighborhood and provide affordable housing there. Other groups had tried but failed to transform the site's historical buildings. At that point, the city of Savannah approached Mercy Housing Southeast to take on this important project. Mercy Housing, St. Joseph/Candler, Mercy Community Capital, and the city of Savannah came together to make it happen.[15]

Sister Betty Walsh RSM, liaison between St. Joseph Chandler Hospital and Mercy Housing, became the champion of revitalizing the area and providing affordable housing for the Cuyler Brownville community. As a native of the city and a former provincial of her religious community who had a wide circle of friends and civic contacts, she possessed a rich understanding of Savannah's needs. In 1999, her research showed that affordable housing was a priority for the city, especially in the Cuyler Brownville area.

Robin Haddock, Mercy Housing South's developer of the project, shares that funding it was really challenging. The initial submission for tax credits was declined because the policy guidelines didn't allow both sites to be considered as one project. Until

Mercy Housing could create a contiguous space by the purchase of two vacant lots adjoining the buildings, such tax credits were not available.[16]

Sister Betty helped provide the information needed to seek historical preservation monies. She did significant research into the historical significance of the buildings, so much so that a heritage display dedicated to her was incorporated into the Heritage Place site.[17] The historical and cultural significance of Charity Hospital and Florence Street School to the city is rooted in the importance they held in the civil rights movement. Both were instruments for addressing the inequities facing African Americans living in Savannah under Jim Crow segregation. Seeking to address educational inequities, leaders of the African American community had pushed for the establishment of Florence Street School. Opened in 1929, it was one of Savannah's early modern public schools for African American students. Newly freed slaves from farms and barrier islands migrated into this area of the city after the Civil War. Dotted with row houses and Victorian single-family dwellings, it captured the spirit of its residents.

Charity Hospital first opened in 1893 as the McKane Training School for Nurses. It transitioned to a hospital for women and children three years later. In 1931, the original hospital was relocated to a new building which was renamed Charity Hospital. It was the first training school for African American nurses and doctors in the Savannah area. Today, Heritage Place and Heritage Corner & Row apartments provide 178 units of housing for the people of the neighborhood, but more than that, they maintain the memory of the heritage which has deep meaning for the community.[18]

Heritage Place was not the only Mercy Housing endeavor that sought to provide needed housing while preserving the legacy of Black heritage and traditions. A second development, Thrive Sweet Auburn in Atlanta, followed the same pattern. In the early 1900s, Sweet Auburn was a place for neighbors to meet and discuss social issues. Sweet Auburn became one of Atlanta's most important historical Black communities.

The area received its name in the 1920s from civil rights activist and businessman John Wesley Dobbs. Dobbs championed voter registration efforts and helped gain Black political power. Dobbs felt that Sweet Auburn reflected the prominence of the area as a national center of Black commerce. Auburn Avenue became a commercial, cultural, and spiritual center for Black life prior to the Civil Rights Movement. Home to the Ebenezer Baptist Church (where the Rev. Dr. Martin Luther King Jr. served as Pastor), the NAACP, Big Bethel A.M.E. Church, and the Royal Peacock Club, where top national performers like Gladys Knight wowed her audiences, the Sweet Auburn neighborhood was a vibrant community witnessing the emergence of the black middle class in Atlanta.[19]

As the civil rights era began to wane, so did the prosperity of the Sweet Auburn neighborhood. With barriers caused by segregation removed, store owners began to move their businesses to Atlanta's west side, and the Sweet Auburn neighborhood went into a period of decline. By 1992, it earned the dubious honor of being named to the top 11 most endangered historical sites in America by the National Trust for Historic Preservation. The character of the area was not only challenged by decline but also by gentrification. Its proximity to the core city and its ease of transportation made the neighborhood attractive to people working in Atlanta's downtown business community.

Behind the scenes, Mercy Housing Inc. had made a commitment to work for culturally appropriate resident policies, and the empowerment of marginalized communities throughout all its properties.[20] Such a commitment was rooted in the Gospel vision that all persons are created in God's image and all persons should be helped to attain the dignity that is rightfully theirs. Partnering with Property Community Connections, Inc. to achieve this was a high priority in the effort to bring affordable housing properties to Sweet Auburn. Reflecting on its commitment to Sweet Auburn, a Mercy Housing publication notes: "Mercy Housing is dedicated to embracing the history this neighborhood is rooted in through our continued work in creating new affordable housing communities within this storied community."[21]

The resulting mixed community that is home to nearly 200 families with low incomes, veterans, and formerly unhoused individuals was not the end of Mercy Housing's effort in the Sweet Auburn area. In partnership with Historic District Development Corporation (HDDC), one of Atlanta's oldest surviving community development corporations and the only nonprofit organization dedicated to preserving affordable housing in the Old Fourth Ward district, Mercy Housing moved forward with the development of a new affordable housing community, Henderson Place. The community is named after Ms. Valena Henderson, a long-time Old Fourth Ward resident and civil rights activist who worked alongside Dr. Martin Luther King Jr. and Ms. Coretta Scott King.

The success of Thrive Sweet Auburn plus Heritage Place and Heritage Corner & Row apartments was a source of celebration for developers and for the communities served. Not all projects proceed as smoothly, however. No matter how much you cultivate a community and gain support of civic leaders, sometimes it is the building itself that can cause developers to lose sleep at night. Such was the case for the Lofts on Arlington, located in the North Lawndale community on the West Side of Chicago. The original building was the historic Sears, Roebuck and Co. catalog printing building. One of the buildings that comprised the vast 55-acre Sears Robuck campus, it sat vacant for 40 years, crumbling into a state of decay. Most of the campus had been re-developed in the 1990's into Homan Square, a mixed-income, low density housing and service-rich neighborhood. What was left unimproved were three commercial buildings including the former Sears, Roebuck & Co Catalog Printing Plant. At its peak, nearly 22,000 people found employment on the campus, many of them Lawndale residents. After the company began phasing out its warehouses and offices in 1974, the area fell into a state of disinvestment, not only taking away jobs but leaving behind a handful of empty, old buildings in its wake.[22]

Walking past a complex of massive red brick buildings every day was a reminder to the community of its loss of jobs, economic stability, and neighborhood prosperity. Mark Angelini, President of Mercy Housing Lakefront, puts that loss this way:

> It became a part of what people saw as the tragedy of North Lawndale that happened from '68 kind of onwards, as the community collapsed after the rioting arising from the assassination of Martin Luther King. The decline really started in the '50s, right as the community was being disinvested, with redlining, phony rent-to-purchase agreements and panic-peddling worked against the needs of the predominately African-American population that was living there.[23]

When Mercy Housing Lakefront took on the task of transforming the abandoned warehouse into 181 affordable apartments, it was not just about preserving a historical building and putting it to good use. Angelini notes that it was about holding on to the industrial architecture in the building while also preserving the unique cultural heritage symbolized by that structure. He shares: "It was great to be able to contribute to preserving something … not only historical from an architectural point of view but also from a cultural and city history point of view." [24]

The transformation was not easy. Obstacles to its fulfillment included everything from a polar vortex which collapsed the roof of the building to an ever-changing political scene in Chicago. Between 2010, when the predevelopment phase started, to 2015, when approvals allowed it to begin, the Chicago Housing Authority changed Directors four times. Each change necessitated starting the conversations all over again. While some directors were favorable, others either wanted the status quo or believed that the proposed plan was untenable. It took time to convince such sceptics that the residents would be safe and have an ordered environment in which to thrive.[25]

A second obstacle was the havoc caused by nature. The polar vortex of 2014 brought both arctic temperatures and massive snow and ice damage to Chicago. Since full access to the building was not possible until after its purchase by Mercy Housing, the unknown damage caused by the vortex was not factored into the development budget. Once inside the building, such damage was vividly evident. Photos of the printing warehouse prior to its rehab show a wide range of derelict conditions —deteriorating inner walls, broken fixtures, fallen ceilings, and litter everywhere — caused by a collapsed roof. The entire top floor of the building had to be stripped down to its supportive columns and water-damaged wood flooring on all the lower floors needed to be replaced.

The damage was so extensive that a choice had to be made on whether to walk away and lose over $1,000,000 in predevelopment costs or to go forward in spite of the additional costs. The choice was to serve the people and provide the affordable housing and the supportive services they needed. The Urban Land Institute awarded Mercy Housing Lakefront and the Lofts its 2020 Jack Kemp Award for the commitment to housing working families in a high-quality, service-enriched property.

Despite the challenges, unexpected delays, and scale of the undertaking, the Lofts on Arlington provided the community with an example of architectural preservation at its best and received a historical preservation award from Landmarks Illinois. But that was not its greatest boast. According to Landmarks Illinois CEO Bonnie McDonald, the special attention that developers gave towards offering support services, while keeping the apartments affordable, played a major role in awarding the preservation award to the Lofts on Arlington: "We're trying to change the narrative about preservation because it's about far more than bricks and mortar. In fact, the reason that we preserve places is for people."[26] McDonald saw the process as one which wove together the past, present, and future in a way that provides supportive, affordable housing. She reflects:

> Demolishing a property really says that the community is not valued ... I think that using this historic building, which is [a] building of great quality, tells the residents that they are valued, that they deserve this quality, they deserve a place that has stood the test of time.[27]

It would be wonderful to think that such unexpected conditions are a one-time occurrence, but that is really not true. Similar conditions emerged when developer Rich Ciraulo worked on the renovation of another historic building in Sacramento, California. Sacramento leaders were eager to retain a balanced amount of single-residency apartments in the downtown area. One of the buildings proposed for such renovation was the old Capitol Park Hotel, built at the turn of the 20th century. Prior to accepting the task of developing the historical building, Mercy Housing developer Rich Ciraulo knew it would be a big job. The hotel rooms lacked cooking facilities and some did not have bathrooms. All that was included in the budget. What was not known was the full extent of the building's deterioration over the years.

No rehabbing of the building had ever occurred. Used by the city as a temporary shelter during the predevelopment period, the plans could only be obtained by laser scanning. No original plans existed. When accessible, it was discovered that the support columns were badly deteriorated, some with big chunks missing. They discovered that the two upper stories of the hotel, added after the original construction, were a "cowboy construction," meaning that no regard was given to the top two floors aligning with the building's structure. Given that the hotel was a historical site, another challenge was to figure out a way that new concrete structures could be connected to the historical brick exterior. Like the experience of the Loft on Arlington, a significant portion of the building had to be gutted before moving forward.

Such problems would discourage any developer, but they were all overcome along the way. Pandemic issues delayed inspections while site visits stretched out the construction schedule. What was harder to resolve, however, was a supply chain failure that delayed electrical components for almost two years. What made it worth all the effort? St. Claire's provides 135 units of permanent supportive housing for formerly homeless persons. Rich Ciraulo points out that it's what Mercy Housing is all about.[28]

In the world of developers, the redesign and renovation of historical buildings is one form of preservation, but the more common mode of preserving housing is the rehabbing of buildings that are beyond their prime. Over the course of time, the buildings tend to deteriorate, causing residents to cope with broken plumbing, unreliable electrical power, and lengthy response times for repairs. Mercy Housing has been involved in preserving such housing complexes since its beginnings. One example is Mercy Magnuson Place in Seattle.

Constructed between 1929 and 1941, a massive three-and-a-half story building, then designated as Building 9, was a bustling barracks housing over 500 Navy squadron members and a mess hall. It was part of the Naval Air Station Sand Point. After the base closed in 1991, the building fell into disrepair. The old barracks evolved into a center for illegal activity, creating safety concerns for everyone: neighbors, park users, and nearby affordable housing communities. That is when Mercy Housing Northwest changed its future.[29]

The newsletter of the Affordable Tax Credit Coalition describes it this way:

> Mercy Housing Northwest envisioned a vibrant, new community housed in a revitalized historic structure where families could thrive and enjoy housing stability often unavailable to lower-income families in Seattle's high-cost housing market. The adaptive reuse and historic preservation of this 250,000 square foot building now provides 148 affordable homes, more than half of which are two- and three-bedroom units, combined with an on-site childcare center and neighborhood health clinic.[30]

The affordable home units are located in the north and south three-and-a-half story residential wings. A six-classroom child-care center, neighborhood health clinic, and spacious community room are situated in the one-and-a-half story center building. The success of the project is witnessed in a statement released by Congresswoman Pramila Jayapa:

> Building affordable housing—and community—is a beautiful and lasting way to preserve an historic landmark. Mercy Housing restored the former U.S Navy Barracks Building 9 into Mercy Magnuson Place, empowering over 100 residents to access affordable housing and thrive in the Magnuson community ...

> These projects provide not only housing, but also access to bustling neighborhoods, outdoor recreation, public transportation and community services. By providing affordable homes coupled with neighborhood access, we are making strides toward realizing housing as a human right. That's why I am so excited for the future of these communities.[31]

Sometimes preserving existing affordable housing units demands creativity. The renovation of Magnuson Place required piecing together funding from ten different funding sources.

Equally demanding of creativity and vision was finding ways to reduce the dynamic of foreclosures that emerged during the great recession of 2008. A major factor in the recession was linked to subprime mortgages, which were home loans granted to borrowers with poor credit histories. The housing boom of the early to mid-2000s led some lenders to be less restrictive in terms of the loans in hopes of capitalizing on rising home prices. It was a disastrous development. As the recession set in, the investment market for subprime mortgages collapsed. Some companies like American Home Mortgage Investment Corp. declared bankruptcy.[32]

Millions of homeowners found themselves "underwater," meaning their homes were valued less than their total loan amounts.[33] Foreclosures on "underwater" homes exacerbated the crisis. In response, the federal government made monies available to get those homes back on the market through the Housing and Economic Recovery Act of 2008 and the American Recovery and Reinvestment Act of 2009, as well as establishing the Neighborhood Stabilization Program.

The government programs gave Mercy Housing a chance to use its expertise, creativity, and passion to help. In 2009, it launched Mercy Portfolio Services, designed to help communities invest the $5 billion they were receiving from the Neighborhood Stabilization Program. Richard Banks, Chief Operating Officer of Mercy Housing at the time, said: "We can help communities realize the benefits of the Neighborhood Stabilization Program by applying Mercy Housing's expertise in real estate development and asset management, so these communities can do the most for their neighborhoods with this funding."[34]

The city of Chicago was quick to act and contracted with Mercy Portfolio Services to acquire and redevelop up to 3,500 properties in its hardest-hit neighborhoods. Not only were properties renovated but local contractors, maintenance workers, and real estate agents were used to carry out the task. The program was phased out in 2015 but had an impressive list of accomplishments. It had preserved, renovated, or facilitated the reoccupation of 2,854 distressed or foreclosed homes over six years. That wasn't all.

It also sustained or created 3,471 jobs and enabled over 7,000 people to benefit from affordable housing.[35]

The largest component of Mercy Housing development is in the sphere of new construction. When Mercy Housing developers create new housing, they are invited into a world of imagination, ingenuity, and professional skill exercised within a circle of relationships. Work done during the pre-development period examines the needs and desires of the community, allowing a new building to incorporate the best of technology and construction while honoring cultural diversity or special needs. Such considerations are vital when providing housing for veterans, many of whom were disabled while serving their country.

Persons with physical disabilities find it difficult to find apartments that meet their needs. Conscious of this need, Mercy Housing develops barrier-free properties which provide accessible, affordable housing for physically disabled residents in an independent living environment. In some complexes, apartments are designed with special accommodations for residents with physical disabilities.

Culturally sensitive design, or architectural designs that fit into a historical neighborhood, challenge imagination. St. Francis Terrace in Sacramento, California. is such a property. Built on land next to the historical Sutter's Fort and St. Francis Church, architects had to revise the original design to match the mission style motif of the area. The small revision won the support of the neighborhood, as well as establishing in the city Mercy Housing's reputation as a developer that listens to and works with the community for the best possible outcomes.

Creating new housing can be a powerful way of addressing marginalized peoples. That is what is happening in Denver, where Mercy Housing is building the city's first apartment complex designed to honor the heritage of American Indian tribes and the need for culturally appropriate services. A circle, a powerful symbol in Native American culture, is the core of the building's design. Carla Respects Nothing has been an important voice in shaping the emerging project. For thirty years, she has worked to reconnect Indian peoples with their culture through "talking circles" organized by the Colorado Coalition for the Homeless, wiping of tears ceremonies for those who have died, and providing opportunities for persons to cook their traditional food. She envisions that such programming will be possible at the new community.[36]

The 187-unit community is housing for all. At the same time, Bill Ziegler, the principal housing consultant for Native American Housing Circle, sees the effort as a significant moment:

> Finally, after a hundred years, it's an opportunity in Denver for American Indian people to live together like historically, we always did," he said. "It gives us an opportunity to heal. It gives us an opportunity to bring each other up and to hold each other accountable and to move forward as a community. It's that shared space together that's going to expedite the healing process.[37]

Shelly Marquez, President of Mercy Housing Mountain Plains, explains that the new Navajo Street development is part of Mercy Housing's focus on addressing housing disparities as well as providing inclusive health and housing services to the residents.[38]

It is evident that developers have to be skilled in multiple areas. They have to be great listeners, problem solvers, and organizers, and skilled at finding adequate funding, but they also have to have an eye on science and innovation. In 2019, as the result of the work done by a project team comprised of Daniel Hernandez, Deanne Tipton, Nick Gormez, and Chris Schmidt, Mercy Housing produced a manual for project managers. It was called "A Manuel for Project Managers: Modular Construction Multifamily Residential Development Type III & Type V Construction."

As one of the leading affordable housing developers in the country, Mercy Housing is continually seeking ways to reduce the time and cost it takes to build affordable housing. The Manual for Project Managers identified multiple ways in which modular construction can reduce construction time, provide an environment free from weather delays during construction, be inspected in the factory, and reduce on-site noise and waste. After researching the potential benefits of various new technologies and approaches, Mercy Housing California decided to focus initially on modular housing. Mercy Housing's first use of the modular construction form has been at two San Francisco projects. Both were selected because of the urgency of providing housing to those unsheltered.[39]

While stewardship of properties and resources has always been a priority within Mercy Housing, so is care of Earth itself. Expanding sustainability practices and strategies across the organization has been part of Mercy's practice since the early 2000s. Sister Lillian Murphy championed the movement, saying: "We believe that sustainably built affordable housing better serves residents by creating healthier environments and reducing energy costs."[40] Residents often struggle to pay for basic utilities. Sustainable practices can significantly lower those costs. Part of Mercy Housing's commitment to sustainability is the introduction of energy audits and the establishment of a baseline measurement of utility consumption for all properties, which can be used to identify where improvements in energy infrastructure are needed.

Mercy Housing's Green Hope Initiative, launched in 2014, guides Mercy Housing in all aspects of operations, from designing, building, and rehabilitating properties to office practices, property operations, and resident services. Jane Graf, Mercy Housing CEO at the time, said: "At Mercy Housing, we believe it is our duty and responsibility to incorporate environmental stewardship principles into all areas of our work … Green Hope will help us create healthy, vibrant communities while also reducing our environmental footprint."[41] To do this, development and construction management staff have created guidelines for future retrofit and new development efforts.

Mercy Housing Mountain Plains shows what kind of innovative work can be accomplished. Working with Energy Outreach Colorado, major energy upgrades were made at six Colorado properties, including everything from pipe insulation to low-flow showerheads. These properties saved more than $75,000 in energy costs while reducing residents' bills between 8% to 28%. Teaming with Mile High Youth Corps, another five Denver properties were able to install water-efficient upgrades with a rebate value of $64,000.[42]

Helped by the American Recovery and Reinvestment Act, Mercy Housing Northwest was able to perform a sweeping retrofit of seven of its multifamily residential properties. Spread throughout Washington State, most of the properties were built around 1975. Mercy Housing Northwest received more than $3.9 million in federal funding to invest in the communities, creating jobs while improving energy efficiency. Mercy Housing's commitment to sustainability has not only saved money and improved the lives of residents, it has been an investment in the future of Earth itself.

No discussion of housing development within Mercy Housing would be complete without including what could be its most formidable challenge, Sunnydale community in San Francisco. To understand the challenge, it is important to know about the community. It was crime-ridden and hope-depleted, isolated and alienated. The housing invited vandalism and despair.

Leslie Fulbright, writing for the San Francisco Chronicle in 2008, reflected:

Such is life in Sunnydale, quite possibly the most dangerous, depressed and decrepit area of the city … Once considered a nice place for a family to live, the development is now home to those who can't afford anything else. There is no landscaping, just overgrown grass and clumps of weeds. There are dirty diapers in trees. Cockroaches and mice run around inside. Some sinks are so moldy, they are black. Walls are crumbling. Stairs have collapsed.

A combination of factors - geographic isolation, extreme poverty and a lack of access to social services - make it virtually impossible to leave Sunnydale. There are no stepping-stones to something better, no road map for how to get out. 'We don't have role models. We don't go to Harvard. We barely have police. We have to take care of ourselves,' said 55-year-old Keith "Kilo" Perry, who runs a barbershop in the development. 'This is like a concentration camp. There is no way out unless you die.'[43]

It is not easy to embrace the call to transformation when conditions are so dire. In addition to the development challenge itself, the risk of failure loomed large. Both lost money and bad publicity were possible if the attempt did not succeed. Jane Graf says that it was one of the difficult choices she ever had to make. "I knew that the Sunnydale development could be one of the most difficult and risky endeavors that myself and Mercy Housing could take on, but probably the most profound work we could do. For those who suggested it was too risky, my reply was, 'That is why we must do this.'"[44]

Saying that it was hard is possibly an understatement. It took 11 years before ground was broken on the project. Since the development required the demolition of the deteriorating homes, priority was given to making sure that current residents were not displaced. The San Francisco Planning website makes that quite clear: "Through the City's HOPE SF Program, [it] will consist of approximately 1,770 residential units (775 replacement affordable units, approximately 200 additional affordable housing units, and approximately 694 market rate units)."[45] Also included in the plan are new streets, utilities, and infrastructure. Space for the community to gather and retail spaces weave together an integrated neighborhood. What is a highlight of the design, however, is the Hub, a community center which provides residents with access to vital onsite services, helps build connections, and creates opportunities for community enhancement.

The whole renovation, estimated to take at least five years, has been guided by the input of the residents themselves. Ashlie Hurst, VP of Community Life at Mercy Housing, sums it up: "The Hub is a testament to Sunnydale's residents' strength, vision, and advocacy. This community center exists because of the countless voices who have spoken up, dreamed big, and worked together to create a space where all can thrive."[46]

What happens at the Hub is the glue that cements the community together. Making sure that happens is the task and mission of Mercy Housing's Property Managers and Resident Service Providers who support the people for whom the ministry exists.

For Your Reflection and Conversation

- Mercy Housing learned over time that not every deal is a good deal. If you were given the task of approving or declining an offer of property for affordable housing, what criteria would you use to decide if it was a "good deal"?

- The rehabbing of a historical building for affordable housing is often more expensive than building a new property. What values or considerations would you see as important in making the decision to choose "preservation" development?

CHAPTER 8

PEOPLE, FIRST, LAST, AND ALWAYS

People are at the heart of the Mercy Housing ministry. It has been that way since the very beginning. Patricia O'Roark was moved to do something because she worked with people experiencing the realities of losing their homes. She saw what it did to families and to children. She heard the stories ripe with fear, hopelessness, and anxiety. They were voices she couldn't ignore. When she approached her religious community, she presented data and an inspiring vision but, more, she called them to act on what they professed, to be Sisters of Mercy reaching out to the most vulnerable.

None of the founding sisters had much expertise in affordable housing but they did have a vast treasure trove of skills in education, administration, healthcare, and social services. They knew people. They knew that just supplying a roof and four walls would not bring families, elders, or persons with special needs the stability, life skills, and self-sufficiency to build new lives and new futures. Sisters like Jeanne Ward and Joan Martin, two of the first sisters to join Mercy Housing, learned quickly that property management was more than repairing buildings and property.

It had to do with transforming lives. It wasn't up to them alone to accomplish such a lofty goal. They had to empower the residents themselves to become invested in their communities and supportive of each other.

In the early years of Mercy Housing Property Management, Sister Libby Fernandez might have symbolized the role. In her assignment as property manager for St. Francis Terrace in Sacramento, she was frequently seen dressed in work clothes with a tool belt around her waist. If something broke, she needed to fix it. If a crisis developed, she worked to resolve it. In a nutshell, the property manager oversaw everything that didn't fall under the job of a developer. No role has changed more during the 40 years of Mercy Housing's existence.

While it was always clear that resident services were critical for residents, how to best structure the ministry to provide such services has been a topic of differing stances over time. When Sister Joan Martin started her ministry at Wylie Street Station in Idaho, she was responsible for everything. The role of resident services didn't exist yet. Sister Terese Tracy had outlined a property manager description that contained over 30 responsibilities. Within that description was an item calling for property managers to "Oversee All Services and Programs."[1] In other words, supervision of resident service providers and the programs offered would be their responsibility.

The type of resident service that might be needed was also described in this early memo which stated that property managers:

> ... insure the provision of housing for the poor while,
> at the same time, offering holistic educational, health,
> and other support programs needed by the poor
> to enable and empower them to control their own

environment and make the major decisions affecting their lives, thus enhancing their dignity as persons and promoting their independence.[2]

Using lived experience as a lens for review, not everyone agreed that this structure was the most effective. Sister Patsy Harney has been part of the Mercy Housing staff for 26 years, primarily serving in resident services. She explains that while working as a team is the ideal, there are times when the property manager and resident services provider might see things very differently. In her view, that is when it is sometimes helpful to have separate lines of reporting. That model can reduce tension and eliminate power-struggle dynamics because the supervisors of each area ultimately resolve the issue.

No matter what model of supervision is used, direct or indirect, what remains a priority is working together for the betterment of each resident and the community as a whole. Ismael Guerrero, President and Chief Executive Officer of Mercy Housing, emphasizes this when he says:

> Our core business, which we excel at, is developing, owning and managing affordable housing; but our mission-work begins when we move a family or individual into their new home. That is where we focus on creating an environment where people thrive, and offer supports that improve health outcomes, economic mobility, and education success. We are committed to making a lasting difference in the communities we serve.[3]

When an individual fails to thrive at a Mercy Housing property, it is sad for everyone involved. In such cases, the property manager has to balance the appropriate implementation of rules and regulations with the well-being of both the individual resident and the resident community. Resident services personnel are primarily focused on supporting residents so they can sustain housing as well as community well-being. There can be differing opinions about what is needed due to varying perspectives. To support both staff and residents at such a time, Mercy Housing has developed a Housing Support Plan which is a multi-step intervention between Property Management and Resident Services.

The first element of the Housing Support Plan is communication. Property Management notifies Resident Service Personnel of lease violation within a 24–72-hour window so that Resident Service Staff can quickly initiate outreach. The structure shows respect for residents by ensuring they are promptly informed and offered the opportunity to address issues before they escalate. This is especially important in vulnerable communities such as refugee populations where proactive education and culturally responsive engagement are essential.

Through Eviction Prevention Coaching, Resident Services staff work to engage residents using empathetic, solution-oriented approaches—developing Housing Support Action Plans or, when necessary, Housing Contracts—to help resolve violations. Weekly collaboration meetings between Property Management and Resident Services reflect a unified, resident-centered approach that upholds mercy in action by prioritizing support over punishment. This aligns with the value of justice, as it ensures equitable access to services and support, particularly for those who may face systemic barriers. Resident Services staff tailor their assistance to each resident's situation—whether financial counseling, hoarding support, or referrals to smoking cessation programs—emphasizing respect for individual dignity and the unique circumstances of each household.

Even when all these actions are taken, some residents are unresponsive and violations continue. An Eviction Prevention Checklist is in place to ensure that all possible resolutions have been explored before final legal steps are taken. This process reflects mercy, offering residents multiple opportunities for support and change before eviction is pursued. Furthermore, it ensures justice by applying consistent procedures and requiring leadership accountability. Throughout all stages, from early intervention to resolution, Mercy Housing's practices reflect a commitment to respect, justice, and mercy, ensuring that housing remains not just a service, but a compassionate and equitable experience for every resident.[4]

An eviction is one of the hardest tasks a property manager must perform. Because Mercy Housing staff are committed to helping residents sustain their housing status, it is hard to terminate housing no matter what the circumstances. The process is never easy. Property managers must follow all the steps required by such a legal process. In addition to federal and state regulations, other regulations may be in play due to the model of funding a property has utilized in its development. Skipping a step in haste can invalidate the eviction.

When all the steps are taken, the process can be lengthy. This is especially troublesome when it is an act of violence that initiates the action. Violence can emerge in diverse modes in any community. Mercy Housing is not exempt from such occurrences, although they are not frequent. Family properties must deal with instances of domestic violence. "Every year, over 10 million cases of domestic violence are reported, with three-quarters of those incidences happening in the home. Given the high volume of rental properties in America, it is inevitable that, at some point, most landlords and tenants are touched by domestic violence."[5]

In such instances, property managers and resident service providers must work together to support and safeguard the victim. Together they must make sure that they obtain written proof that the tenant is a victim of domestic violence, help obtain a restraining order to prevent the abuser from returning and do such things as change locks, or allow the victim to terminate a lease early in order to escape. All this is needed to successfully evict the abuser and protect the victim. Many women who seek affordable housing are women who have fled abusive situations and find themselves in need of safe housing for themselves and their children.

One such resident, Rahel, found herself in such circumstances. Fearful for the safety of her small children, who were two and five, she left her home. Even though she had no fallback plan, she needed to leave her job in order to escape completely. When Rahel was able to connect with Mercy Housing Northwest through her social worker, she was able to begin again. As she puts it: "Relief came in a home. Walking through the doors of my apartment …, I felt absolute relief that my kids had a safe place to sleep."[6]

With the support she received from the Resident Services team, Rahel returned to school, moved to King County Housing, and earned her nursing degree. She became a homeowner and saw her oldest child begin college at Harvard University. Her story sums up what Mercy Housing is about. As a staff member of Mercy Housing Northwest puts it:

> At Mercy Housing Northwest, we believe that homes give people strength. A safe, clean, affordable home designed with equity and dignity in mind is a foundation from which life can blossom. Robust and enriched services targeted at the needs and aspirations of residents of all ages can change lives.[7]

In a society that has escalating violence, unexpected things can happen. Staff members can be attacked or threatened. One can never predict when a circumstance may trigger an episode of PTSD in a tenant or staff member, which then must be de-escalated. Mercy Housing's properties that welcome the mentally ill or chronically unsheltered are particularly vulnerable to such occurrences.

While tragic events are not an everyday occurrence at Mercy Housing properties, when one does occur it reminds us that property management is difficult and challenging, as are resident services. Dedication to helping the most vulnerable provides no shield from backlash, hostility, and unprovoked verbal or physical abuse. Providing an environment that is welcoming, safe, and beautiful does not mean that residents will respect it and tend it, although most do. Some residents come from very traumatic and violent lived experiences and have chronic and severe mental health and substance abuse issues. These can create barriers to tenancy and often result in lease violations. Lack of attention or even deliberate intent can result in flooded apartments. Lack of cleanliness, or destructive acts, are frustrating because they consume both time and resources. Such situations can be discouraging and require lots of patience and inner calm to address. Ramie Dare sums it up with the words: "We do hard."[8]

While crisis events garner the headlines, the everyday responsibilities of property managers and resident service providers are challenging in different ways. Property managers have a formidable list of tasks. Responsibilities for property managers at Mercy Housing span 15 separate categories which have 77 tasks identified. Just a few illustrate the scope of the position. There are oversight responsibilities such as inspection of the property, identifying safety hazards or property damage, and then making sure those issues are addressed. Making sure that the property and its residents are following regulations set forth by federal, state, and local agencies — as well the funders — is core to the property manager's role.[9]

The property manager also has to be a sales representative, greeting, assisting, and qualifying prospective residents. Properly vetting prospective residents carries great importance because accepting someone who is a danger to other residents, or is beyond what the community can support, can lead to problems going forward. Here the property managers' familiarity with all regulatory agreements and related agencies helps to ensure 100% compliance with all regulations. This includes all the fair housing regulations, sexual harassment laws, disability accommodations, HUD and Tax Credit guidelines, and the landlord-tenant relationship guidelines of Mercy Housing itself. No property manager can do all this without support and collaborative partners.

Another aspect of property management is financial. The manager must assist in the collection of all money due to Mercy Housing for rents, damages, late fees, etc., and the preparation of receipts. When that doesn't happen according to plan, the manager has to follow up on collections, delinquent rents, and un-honored checks. This is in addition to being able to manage finances and work within a budget.

A particularly challenging aspect of all this is what is called economic occupancy. What that means in practice is that the budget of a property is projected based on full occupancy. When that fails to be a reality, budget gaps can occur. Vacant apartments are financially challenging. Property managers must see that vacancies are filled within a tight window. According to Mercy Housing's operational manual, they must be ready for occupancy within three to seven days depending on their size.

A flooding apartment that leaks through to the apartment below means that the property manager must not only see that the damage is addressed quickly but must also address the issue of relocation. Jacquie Hoffman, Senior Vice President of Property Operations, Mercy Housing Management Group, points out that residents are encouraged to carry renter's insurance for just such situations. When dislocation happens, the Red Cross frequently partners with Mercy Housing to assist the dislocated residents. If an on-site apartment is available, then a quick solution for relocation can happen. Jacquie shares that, although not required to do so, Mercy Housing does everything possible to help residents find housing because that is part of its mission.[10]

Perhaps one of the most challenging tasks the property manager must handle is to remain calm, focused, and rational in emergency situations. Emergencies can and do take multiple forms — equipment failures, accidents, health emergencies, and violent incidents all require a professional response. It is also a time when the property manager's ability to build networks of support is most in play. They need to know who to call and have confidence that help is going to arrive in a timely manner.

The property manager is also responsible for implementing ministry-wide initiatives such as Mercy Housing's Green Hope initiative. While developers are responsible for designing buildings with energy-efficient equipment, property managers and resident service coordinators are charged with encouraging "energy and water conservation and sustainable habits among residents via behavior change prompts/flyers."[11] It isn't easy to foster a property-wide community that values environmental sustainability and works to practice such things as composting, water and energy conservation, and repurposing.

Crossroad Gardens in Sacramento is an example of how change comes about. In 2018, major renovation was completed for the property. Solar panels, upgraded windows, and an energy-efficient heating and cooling system were installed. The goal was to reduce energy costs for residents while contributing to earth sustainability. Hannah Wolfe, resident services coordinator for the property, relates that the residents have been delighted with the results. Roosevelt Williams, a Crossroad Gardens resident, tells us: "I'm on a fixed income. With the upgrade, everything seems like it is a little bit lower and it helps out a lot."[12] Energy costs have decreased. The reduction in costs, as well as in energy usage, has allowed residents to feel greater freedom in using air conditioning during Sacramento's frequent 100°F summer weather.

Communication and negotiation skills are vital to the success of property management. The property manager must supervise the maintenance staff as well as any additional Mercy Housing Management Group staff that work at the property. Prior to 2005, that included resident service providers. Supervision is one place where communication is essential, but such skills are also important in building relationships with the surrounding neighborhood, civic officials, and partners in the effort to provide supportive housing for those who need it.

It is not an exaggeration to say that the property manager is the face of Mercy Housing for the residents as well as for the neighborhood. The Property Resource Guide and Agreement for Mercy Housing states that "in all cases, the execution of property management responsibilities is intended to uphold Mercy Housing's core values of Respect, Justice and Mercy for our residents, partners, and the larger community."[13] To do this consistently and vigorously requires that the core values of Mercy Housing be owned by the managers in mind and action. As the Partnership Resource Guide puts it, the values will permeate "throughout our partnerships, operations, and interactions."[14] The Resource Guide also makes explicit what that means:

> **Respect:** A basic perspective and behavior which is attentive, considerate and shows special regard for the inherent dignity of persons and the sacredness of creation.

> **Justice:** Ensure equal access, opportunity and mobility for all by identifying and eliminating obstacles that prevent full participation in community.

> **Mercy:** The ability to see need and respond with compassion.[15]

Embracing these core values provides a model of how staff deals with residents. It overflows into the legal responsibilities that are part of the job for both property managers and resident service coordinators. Seeing that Fair Housing norms are implemented is an integral part of acting on Mercy Housing's core values, and a critical component of an equitable model for delivering customer services. Creation of a welcoming environment for all, managing consistently to enforce regulatory standards without special treatment, and documenting everything is essential. Failure to tend the issues of liability and standards can result in legal action against staff and/or Mercy Housing, discrimination complaints, and more. Such occurrences are costly and time-consuming as well as draining for the staff.[16] From a mission perspective, failure to implement Fair Housing norms also violates the spirit of Mercy Housing's mission.

Two additional implications flowing from the core values are collaboration and empowerment. In order to achieve Mercy Housing's national impact goals of housing success and Health and Wellness, people have to work together: staff and residents.

This philosophy is reflected in the blended management style that permeates the management structure of Mercy Housing. The style is defined as "a collaborative partnership between Mercy Housing Management Group and Resident Services working in a spirit of cooperation and responsibility to achieve our mission and ensure resident stability."[17] Blended management provides a model of working together that is experiential, not just conceptual. The need for collaboration between property managers and resident service coordinators has been recognized since the beginning of Mercy Housing. The first sister managers advocated separating the functions. It was a simple case of recognizing that one person was not able to provide the full range of services needed for successful, affordable housing property management and resident empowerment. The roles required different skill sets and expertise. A review of the job description for resident service coordinators quickly illustrates the difference.

Like the property manager, the resident service coordinator is called to uphold Mercy Housing's core values as they relate to residents and the larger community. There is no cookie cutter model for resident services. Mercy Housing has three distinct types of housing communities. The first is family housing, which was the original focus of the ministry. The guiding question was: "What is needed for this family to flourish?" Things like after-school programs for children, parenting support, help finding employment, and financial literacy were all part of the early mix.

When Mercy Housing joined with Catholic Charities Housing, San Francisco, the merger changed the mix because the portfolio Catholic Charities Housing brought into Mercy Housing was primarily senior housing. Resident services had to adapt to new needs and new possibilities. While some seniors might not have financial resources, they have life experience and talents to contribute. The creation of Strategic Healthcare Partners brought a health and wellness aspect that was especially important for senior communities.

The third housing model, special needs supportive housing, also found its origins in the portfolio of Catholic Charities Housing, San Francisco. Since that time, Mercy Housing has recognized that there are unique housing challenges for some populations like veterans, the chronically unsheltered, as well as persons with mental illness. Often people on the edge of homelessness descend into depression and addiction when misfortune or loss of employment causes them to lose their housing. Moving from a home to living in their car is, for many, a recipe for hopelessness.

One example of what can happen when resident service personnel, property managers, and outside collaborators come together to provide housing stability and support is the story of Marisol Taberez. A combination of substance abuse and mental health challenges brought her to homeless shelters. Her family moved her to Sacramento, away from her negative environment. In 2009, after reaching sobriety for six years, she was given a chance to move into Mercy Housing California's Martin Luther King, Jr. Village, one of a dozen supportive housing properties managed by Mercy Management Group in the Sacramento area. At the time, Jane Graf shared: "We have a serious commitment to helping individuals break the cycle of chronic homelessness. We can't do it alone. In collaboration with other great agencies in Sacramento, we are finding solutions."[18]

> For Marisol, finding housing at Martin Luther King
> Jr. Village was her solution. I love my new home
> because it's mine. When I first walked up to my

house, I said 'this is my own key. I get to open my own door.' I don't have to sleep in a park or in a bathroom stall. I don't have to worry about anything anymore.[19]

With safety and stability, she has begun training to be a drug and alcohol counselor for others. "In a million years I never thought I could become a drug counselor. All the people here who have helped me are just tremendous. I can now walk with my head up instead of down."[20]

Working together, resident services and property management share responsibility for housing stability, success, and retention. They also come together to help plan resident meetings or Community Connect meetings which deepen resident engagement, foster leadership from community members, or build relationships. Community Connect meetings, in particular, are resident-centered.[21] Since every type of property is different, programming varies and responding to that diversity is a special focus of resident services.

Empowerment of residents and community engagement are key to creating thriving communities. The residents of all modes of Mercy Housing possess talents, skills, and insight that contribute to the creation of a community that really cares for each other. When that happens, good things happen. Diane Kock is an example of such a resident. She lives in a mixed community of 154 families and senior homes at Mercy Housing Crestview Village in LaVista, Nebraska. When she moved into the property with her two children, she noticed that few residents socialized or got to know each other. That was not the kind of community she wanted to have so she set about changing it. She planned property events and organized chili suppers and other intergenerational events. She spent time talking with senior residents and understanding their interests.

Diane's work has changed the community. Children shovel snow for elders and carry their groceries. People now socialize after work. They look out for one another as they continue to become a vibrant community. The effort has changed Diane as well. Her service has expanded her organizational skills, inspired her to higher goals, and helped her to become open to discussing problems. It has also given her a future vision: to work in a retirement center or a senior living facility.[22]

Twenty-five years later, the spirit of community envisioned by Diane for Crestview Village finds its expression through the Neighbor-Up program which makes a difference every day. The program itself was founded in August 2020 as a response to the pandemic. Dawn, an 11-year resident of Crestview Village, joined with ten other residents in accepting the role of a Neighbor-Up leader. Resident volunteers lead the program with the goal of bringing neighbors together to find creative solutions to issues that challenge the community.[23] Their efforts range from providing community snow shovels and ice melt to creating welcome baskets for new residents. Food trains are arranged for families in need, and a walking group has been formed to promote wellness. Keeping the community safe, helping fulfill needs and providing support are at the heart of the program. Crestview Village's Resident Services Coordinator provides the help and support to organize the resident-led monthly meetings. Dawn says: "You have to love people right where they are at, not where they want to go or where they have been."[24]

Crestview Village was not the only Mercy Housing property that had to creatively respond to the demands of the pandemic. Every property in every region of the ministry had to do so, and both resident service staff and property management rose to meet the unexpected needs of the moment. Jane Graf worked at keeping everyone informed, but even more, inspired while moving through the difficult time. In speaking to the whole staff, she shared not only her gratitude but her awe of the way in which everyone responded. "I've seen the compassion, the dedication, the creativity, the unbelievable creativity. It's inspiring."[25] She spoke of not only the massive efforts at the properties, but also the enormous work behind the scenes where supplies had to be found, bills paid, development efforts continued, and funds raised.

A quick glance at the communications sent out during the pandemic reveal an attention to every aspect of the community, with detailed information about what actions needed to be taken when situations occurred. Such advice was not limited to tasks. Some advice had to do with nurturing the human spirit. Jane said:

> As you adjust to a new normal and navigate challenges in these uncertain times, I want to remind you that you are needed. You are strong. And we are in this together... Thank you for all the acts of kindness that happen each and every day. As we go through this together, remember to stop, breathe, and connect with each other. Together we are making a difference.[26]

Efforts in the Pacific Northwest are a snapshot of what the whole of Mercy Housing experienced and the vital role that resident services played in keeping residents safe and healthy. Like all Mercy resident services across the country, Mercy Housing Northwest was rapidly pivoting and learning about what the Covid-19 pandemic meant for the communities served. As a housing organization, shelter-in-place took on new resonance. Working together, property managers and resident service coordinators had to find new ways of holding the community together. New challenges arose. Ways of connecting to the resident community changed overnight and it was quickly apparent that onsite services provided a lifeline to residents.[27]

Meeting the needs of residents during this overwhelming time meant connecting kids and parents to their teachers and administrators, ensuring computer support was available along with adequate internet access. For seniors, there had to be increased wellness checks to reduce isolation, anxiety, and depression as residents were socially distanced. The economic impact was another reality. A blog about these times, "COVID-19 Response: Recovery and Resilience," is posted on the Mercy Housing website and describes the efforts:

> We helped residents, rocked by the economic impact of coronavirus, to apply for unemployment benefits, secure stimulus payments and file taxes. In a matter of weeks, the Resident Services teams' efforts to connect residents with food increased tenfold. We leveraged corporate donations, food bank partnerships, and onsite community spaces to ensure residents would have access to food during these challenging times.[28]

It required lots of partnerships and civic community involvement to make all this happen. One of the creative partnerships was the Community Kitchens for Affordable Housing Residents, a partnership of four entities which have local restaurants provide meals for residents of King County communities. The funding was provided through a Covid-19 response grant from Bank of America Foundation. Other partnerships, such as one with Safeway's Nourishing Neighbors grant program, allowed food access programming through the end of 2020.

Coming together in the initial months of the pandemic allowed Mercy Housing to provide a vigorous response in the face of need. Numbers from the Mercy Housing Northwest region tell the story:

> Resident Services devoted 4,500 services to keep youth busy –– including educational support, enrichment activities, social and emotional learning opportunities, and recreation.

> In just five months, the Resident Services team provided more than 35,000 food services!

> Thanks to Capital One, 148 tablets with internet service plans were provided to Mercy Magnuson Place residents.[29]

One major pandemic challenge — food insecurity — was not new to resident service coordinators. It has been a constant in the lives of 21st-century Americans. The Department of Agriculture estimates that 46.3% of American adults are food insecure.[30]

In 2020, the percentage of adults that had inadequate food was under 8% but by 2023, that percentage grew to 12.5%. People simply couldn't afford the cost of food.[31] Given the fact that residents at Mercy Housing properties are financially pressed, helping to connect them to food resources is important to their well-being. Resident service coordinators have been creative in finding partnerships and pathways to greater food access.

At Mercy Housing Northwest's Mercy Magnuson Place, the issue of healthy food access was a major concern. Although the center has an onsite health clinic, childcare center, and resident services programming, it existed in a food desert. The nearest option for groceries was the convenience foods found at the 7-Eleven across the street. After months of planning and collaboration, the Magnuson Park Community Food Pantry was launched with the help of four community partners.

Between its start in August 2019 and January 2020, the Food Pantry, hosted on-site, served 330 households and distributed over 35,000 pounds of food to Mercy Housing residents and the surrounding community. It was possible because of collaboration. The University District Food Bank provides the food, the YMCA provides volunteers to assist, Solid Ground staff members hold cooking demonstrations showing how pantry food can be used, while Mercy Magnuson Place provides the venue.[32]

All the creative ways that have been implemented to access food have helped to reduce food insufficiency, but food scarcity remains and impacts those who experience it. That reality moved Mercy Housing to collaborate with the Nutrition in Housing pilot program, Share Our Strength's No Kid Hungry. The initiative, aimed at addressing food scarcity in food deserts, was implemented at three Mercy affordable housing sites in Esparto, CA; Stockton, CA; and Savannah, GA. Parag Gupta, Chief Program Officer for Mercy Housing shares: "This program proves that addressing food insecurity within affordable housing communities is not only doable but also highly successful. This creative collaboration enhanced the food environment through local partnerships that provided direct access to nutritious food through food pantries, food delivery services, and youth programs; and growing food in community gardens."[33] The pilot provided four learnings:

- Leveraging Supplemental Nutrition Assistance Program benefits and innovative food delivery services like Instacart Health Fresh Funds, along with community gardens and food pantries, allowed families access to fresh and healthy food as well as increasing their food supply.

- Local residents taking on the role of "wellness champions" play a key role in organizing nutrition classes, tending community gardens, and connecting families to food resources. Programs helped empower the residents to take a more active role in their own health and nutrition.

- Assisting families in accessing SNAP benefits greatly increased access to additional food. Assistance in navigating application and renewal processes helped achieve a 70% enrollment level for eligible residents.

- As food security increased, stress lessened. Over half of the participants noted higher energy levels, reduced stress and better overall well-being.[34]

Healthcare leaders have long known that there exists a critical link between health and lack of adequate housing. Persons who are unsheltered or inadequately sheltered lack the environment which nurtures healing and good health. That connection is highlighted in the story of Steve Allen. His substandard housing brought him to the cusp of being incapacitated. Deplorable might be a word to describe his housing situation. Steve shares: "The conditions were horrible. There were holes in the floor, no maintenance and constant fighting and hollering outside my apartment."[35] Things got worse. One night when getting up to get a glass of water, Steve stepped on a nail in his deteriorating floor. He contracted blood poisoning but couldn't afford to see a doctor. "After five days of hallucinating and excruciating pain, Steve finally realized he needed to call 9-1-1."[36]

The result of his delay was the amputation of his leg.

Without other resources, Steve had to return to his home. Worrying about what would happen next increased his mental distress. Finally, his rent was raised and he was forced to leave. It was then that he found Mercy Riverside, a Mercy Housing property in Red Bluff. A year and a half later, Steve saw a big change in both his health and his perspective. Mercy Housing's affordable rent allowed him to have money for both medical expenses and regular living costs. The collaboration with Strategic Heathcare Partnership helped him access affordable healthcare services and counseling. He got the support he needed to change his life. As Steve puts it: "Having a safe place that cares what happens to me makes all the difference. I am happier and healthier."[37]

The important connection of health and housing is reflected in housing design over the last two decades. On-site clinics are sometimes built into the design of the property from the beginning. Neither property managers nor resident service staff are medical personnel, but they are connectors. The mode of collaboration varies across the country. In some cases, commercial space is designed to accommodate the needs of a clinic which is then leased and run by third-party agencies. In other cases, collaboration between Mercy Housing properties and providers of medical or social services create opportunities for such providers to come on-site to serve the residents. Though taking different forms, resident service personnel act as a type of medical navigator, helping residents access the care they need and supporting them as they seek to become healthier.

What can be done in the area of health is shown by the accomplishments of Mercy Housing Mountain Plains region. In 2014, they were able to have two-thirds of their properties access needed health and wellness programs and services. Five Colorado properties established Health Navigator Programs funded by grants from Caring for Colorado Foundation and Enterprise Community Partners. The grants allowed Mercy Housing to work with community health providers, offering such things as on-site health screenings for chronic health issues, vaccinations, and assistance in enrolling in health insurance options.

Properties in Arizona focused on helping their senior communities. Mercy Housing Mountain Plains partnered with Grand Canyon University Nursing School to provide basic health screening, assist seniors with medication management, and encourage physical activity. Children were not left out. Two of the largest properties in Omaha focused on physical activity in their after-school program which served 180 children. Physical activity is not the only service provided to children at Mercy Housing family properties. There are many programs designed to contribute to the growth and development of youth of any age.

From the beginning of the ministry, many of the early property managers were sister educators like Sister Jeanne Ward. They were well aware of what was needed to help children thrive. Resident service coordinators like Sister Patsy Harney keep that focus alive. An advocate for the importance of technology access for children and adults, Sister Patsy was instrumental in Mercy Housing's initiative to set up seven technology centers funded by a grant from the Department of Education. Such centers, now a constant in design, make it possible for children to keep up with their classes. Jack Diepenbrock, a former Mercy Housing Inc. Board member, echoes Sister Patsy's concern for children. "I think you can make the biggest difference by helping the children. To rescue a kid from abject poverty and give them tools like after-school programs — that's what makes a difference in a community."[38]

Sterling Meadows community in the Mercy Housing Northwest

region is an example of what can happen when kids get the help they need. Over a ten-year period, the graduation rate of their resident children went from zero to 95%. Among the approaches used are Homework Club, connection with teachers of the students, and the Mercy Scholars Program. Sometimes it's not programs but supplies that matter.

The estimated cost of "back to school" expenses for one child in 2022 was $661.[39] For families who have to choose between food and school supplies, the choice usually falls to food. That choice can have long-term consequences since not having school supplies puts kids at a disadvantage, seriously impacts their learning, and continues a cycle of poverty that decreases their chance of reaching their full potential. Recognizing that reality, Mercy Housing Mountain Plains organized a backpack drive for their children across all its properties.

In addition to after-school programs, day-care centers, tutoring, and computer labs, resident service staff use a variety of creative ways to enhance the education of children. Field trips, reading clubs, and special educational programs are all part of the mix. Mercy Housing Mountain Plains (MHMP) and community partner the Young Americans Bank joined together to offer an entrepreneurial program for youth residents in grades 6 through 12. The idea was to teach kids about becoming entrepreneurs through experience. The hands-on program called YouthBiz is sponsored by Young Americans Bank. For ten weeks, each participant is challenged to create a business from concept to completion. Among the skills learned were the importance of critical thinking, collaboration, communication, taking the initiative, information literacy, creativity, and accountability.[40] It also was fun.

Educational opportunities for adult residents follow a slightly different path. Adults know what they want to learn, what they enjoy, and what they don't. Community Connect encourages residents to be part of the decision-making process when it comes to programming. While fiscal skills, cooking classes, and sobriety programs are important options, participation depends on the interest of the residents. They are most effective when they are offered in response to requests from the residents themselves.

Childcare programs and after-school activities help parents to seek out for themselves the educational opportunities previously blocked by lack of childcare.

Providing support to adults who want to improve their lives through education is an important part of helping them to reshape their lives. The impact of such support and encouragement is reflected in the number of Mercy Housing staff that are former or current residents. The transformation that can happen is captured in the story of Sarah Peralta. Sarah has been an employee of Mercy Housing for almost 20 years and currently is Senior Resident Services Coordinator at two Mercy Housing properties in Folsom, California. But things were not always this way. Sarah and her children moved to Folsom to be close to her husband who was incarcerated at Folsom Prison. She moved into an apartment complex that was commonly called "Prison Wife Row." Faced with multiple emotional and economic challenges, she was determined to have a more stable life for herself and her children.

In 1997, Mercy Housing California purchased and rehabilitated the run-down apartment complex where she lived. That is when things began to turn around. Encouraged by Mercy Housing staff, Sarah signed up for programs that could improve her situation: things like resume workshops and a GED program as well as a homebuyer's program. She later moved to Folsom Gardens, another Mercy Housing property nearby. Having succeeded in earning her GED and in purchasing her own mobile home, Sarah says: "In my life, no one ever had believed in me. Everyone shuts you out when you're a prison family … but the staff at Folsom Gardens really [invested] in me. They said, 'Sarah, you can do it,' and they believed in me. If you knew me before and you know me now, you'd see I'm a different person."[41]

Sarah continued her studies and worked hard in various financial stability programs. Her natural ability to form relationships with residents, and her experience, made her an ideal candidate for employment at Mercy Housing. Alvin Tuvilla, MHC's Vice President of Resident Services, recognized her potential and asked her to apply for a job on his team. Twenty years later, she is still giving back to others what she received: support, encouragement, and a belief that they can claim a better future.

Mercy Housing's founding religious were dedicated to helping people overcome their past difficulties and begin again. Whether it was an abused woman escaping domestic violence or a recovering addict, they worked to help that person find a new beginning by providing shelter and support. For many, that support and shelter is not easy to access. One of the populations that often find it hard to begin again are persons who are transitioning from incarceration to normal life. They face many challenges. Michael Boyd knows first-hand. He spent over 30 years in prison before he had a chance to begin anew.

Michael says: "I knew I was going to have challenges. When a person comes from prison a lot of times housing is denied to them because of their background. Landlords think that you are going to be a problem not knowing that people have changed."[42] Determined to move forward despite the challenges, Michael sought support at Safer Foundation, an organization that helps justice-involved people gain stability.

A partnership between Safer Foundation and Mercy Housing Lakefront made it possible for Michael to move into the South Loop Apartments, a Mercy Housing Lakefront supportive housing community. It was facilitated by a Master Lease program between the two organizations. By the master lease, Mercy Housing Lakefront is able to house individuals who have begun recovery from their traumas in a permanent setting while they continue to receive their program of services from Safer.[43]

Having the support of both Safer Foundation and Mercy Housing Lakefront's onsite case management services helped Michael move forward successfully. He enjoys life with the senior community of which he is a part as well as spending time with his grandchildren. Grateful for a second change at life and the stability of a home, Michael is focused on what matters most to him. His relationship with his family.

Running through every program and procedure are the core values of Mercy Housing: Respect, Justice and Mercy. At the heart of property management and resident services are the goals of empowerment and community. While community events, meaningful engagement, and an experience of being valued are vital, Mercy Housing leaders and Board members recognized that more was needed. That "more" takes the shape of Mercy Together: Our Differences Make the Difference as an initiative that could bring the vision to reality. It was shaped by the long-held understandings which guide action.

Mercy Housing has always believed that having varied perspectives helps generate better ideas to solve the complex housing challenges of a changing — and increasingly diverse — country; that its over-all culture should reflect the kind of community its wants to see by including people from any number of demographic backgrounds and identities and valuing the collective strength of their experiences, beliefs, values, skills, and perspectives; that healthy communities are a result of creating an environment of involvement, respect, and connection — where the richness of ideas, backgrounds, and perspectives are valued.[44]

Ismael Guerrero summarized what Mercy Together expresses in a letter to Mercy Housing staff. He outlined it in five key points:

> Mercy Together affirms our commitment to our core values of Respect, Justice and Mercy as envisioned by our Founding Communities of women Religious. It guides our dedication to creating a workplace and communities where everyone feels valued and has equal access to opportunities.

> Mercy Together calls on employees, residents, and partners to come together to celebrate our differences and leverage our unique perspectives and experiences. We aim to create a welcoming, open community where everyone feels valued and can contribute fully.

> Mercy Together strives to build bridges across our differences, foster collaboration, create inclusive practices and ensure access to opportunities for all. Together, we can build a future where every person, regardless of their identity or background, is treated fairly and we succeed together.

> Mercy Together pledges to explore the roots of historic injustices, address economic disparities in our communities, and speak the truth about the lived experiences of Mercy Housing residents and staff. Our founding communities of Women Religious envisioned

a just world and set our housing ministry on the path to be relentless advocates for housing justice.

Mercy Together commits to being a humble, learning organization. Mercy Housing aims to enhance awareness and understanding to make decisions that help employees and residents thrive. We know we can do better in changing our practices, policies, and the world, to attain better outcomes for everyone.[45]

Sometimes it is easy to write an inspiring vision only to find that it fails to come to realization. To make sure that the vision put forth in Mercy Together becomes concrete, Mercy Housing's Strategic Plan for 2024 to 2026 includes concrete, measurable steps toward creating a ministry-wide movement which matches words with deeds. Mercy Together acted upon the strategic business plan priorities by bringing people together to learn and grow from different perspectives; focusing on better solutions and outcomes; involving more interested parties in decision-making through regional Together teams and leveraging our differences as a strength not a liability.[46]

Translating this vision into everyday practice is not a new development. It began in the Mercy Housing Lakefront region in 2000. The region worked to support values of inclusion because it believed that "embracing diversity provides for a stronger community in which to work and live."[47] In the Mercy Housing Northwest region, this effort at including everyone has taken flesh through its resident translators, known as Language Liaisons. Resident Services Coordinator Natalie Kotar notes: "Having resident interpreters helps me more efficiently oversee the programs."[48] Throughout its properties, 32 primary languages are spoken, everything from Amharic to Spanish, Oromo to Yap. The addition of headphones providing simultaneous translation has resulted in greater participation across the resident community. Using such tools at Community Connect provides a way in which residents of all cultures can share their insights and concerns.

Whether it is hosting an international night, sharing ethnic foods or customs, or building culturally sensitive properties, Mercy Housing seeks to welcome persons of all backgrounds and ethnicities. One example of honoring cultural diversity is a Mercy Housing property on Navaho Street in Denver The new building, designed to honor the cultural contributions of American Indian and Alaskan peoples, is also an effort to address the housing disparities experienced by indigenous peoples. According to Adrianne Maddux, executive director of Denver Indian Health and Family Services, Native Americans suffer from some of the worst health disparities in the world. "Native Housing is a well-known contributor to health outcomes and a meaningful lever for health equity. We have provided culturally responsive services to the native community for over 45 years. This opportunity is a positive step in honoring and supporting our native community."[49]

Story after story affirms that Mercy Housing changes lives, one by one. The stories tell of hopelessness transforming into hope, of fear changing into inner freedom. Parag Gupta calls it "the greatest story never told."[50] Chuck Wehrwein, Senior Vice President in 2004, puts it a different way: "When you see the impact that affordable, stable housing makes in a person's life, especially those with special needs, then you realize there is just no greater calling than that. Every resident I meet gets me to go out and work harder. This work really makes a difference."[51] That is what property managers and resident service coordinators are all about: making a difference that changes lives. Continuing this vision and mission is what prompted the transition of Mercy Housing, Inc. to a "legacy ministry," a governance structure that would ensure that the values of the founding sisters would endure into the future.

• •

For Your Reflection and Conversation

- The well-being of residents is at the heart of Mercy Housing's mission. Demands on property managers and resident services staff are constant. What do you believe is needed to support, strengthen, and renew the Mercy Housing personnel in those roles?

- Two of the key elements fostered within the Mercy Housing properties are community and empowerment. How can these qualities best be fostered? How are networking systems part of that effort?

BEYOND TODAY, A COMMITMENT TO LIVE THE LEGACY

"Since 1981, Mercy Housing has helped provide affordable, safe, and stable homes for more than 250,000 people in 45 states and Puerto Rico." Those are the words on Mercy Housing's Website that capture its impact on people and communities since its beginning. Today, Mercy Housing, Inc. is a legacy ministry, meaning that it has committed itself to carry on the values, vision, and mission that it inherited from its founding religious communities. It is a legacy to celebrate and to tend.

In order to adapt to changing relationships and needs, Mercy Housing's governance structures changed to ensure that the organization remained fiscally healthy while remaining faithful to the legacy it has received. Its founders realized that their memberships were diminishing, and changes had to take place to insure that the legacy would be carried into the future. Thus they sought to embrace a structure that would be rooted in its values and nimble enough to adapt to the changing needs of each new decade. How the structures evolved is a witness to the desire for the ministry to continue as long as there is need.

When Sister Terese Tracy founded the ministry in 1981, its structure was similar to that used by healthcare systems of the time. It had two parts: a corporate member group and a board. When Sister Lillian Murphy became CEO of Mercy Housing in 1986, she had two key concerns: the growth and the sustainability of the Housing ministry. Her task was not just about growing the ministry and making sure it was sustainable. It was about mission, about providing the person-centered type of housing envisioned by its religious founders.

Although recognized as a Catholic entity due to its listing in the Official Catholic Directory, Mercy Housing is, in fact, a civil corporation. Canon lawyers over the years assured Mercy Housing leadership that the ministry has no canonical status, is not a juridic person, and its property is not considered ecclesiastical so it is not subject to canon law.[1] A question which was always in the minds of Mercy Housing's leadership was what kind of structure was needed to allow it to be nimble, flexible, and effective going forward.

In the initial years of Mercy Housing, the founding religious communities — many of which sponsored healthcare institutions — were familiar with the Corporate Member/Board of Trustee structure. While the Board was responsible for oversight of operations, including strategic plans, mission adherence, and financial well-being, the Corporate Members held what were called "reserved rights." Those rights included such things as acceptance of new sponsors, defining the mission of the ministry, and approval of a new CEO and Board appointments. In other words, the Corporate Members had the highest level of authority, called for accountability, and had the final approval of any major changes to the vision.

In 1981, when Mercy Housing was formed, the Leadership Team for the Sisters of Mercy of Omaha comprised the whole

Corporate Member Group. By 1996, when more religious communities became co-sponsors of the ministry, that Corporate Member Group had grown to 12, with each co-sponsoring community having two sisters in the group. As more communities became co-sponsors, the size of the group became unwieldy. A committee was formed to evaluate the structure and make recommendations. It was the beginning of a series of small structural revisions like reducing religious co-sponsor representation on the Corporate Member Group to one member each.

While conversations and options about governmental structure continued, no major changes were made until 2004 when the Articles of Incorporation and Bylaws were revised to delegate to the Mercy Housing Incorporated Board the reserved rights of the Corporate Member Group that governed business decisions. This was done to protect the Corporate Member Group from legal and financial liability. The question of governance structure continued to arise. Four years later, the structure changed again. A Sponsorship Council of one representative from each of the sponsoring communities was created. The Corporate Member Group was reduced to three representatives selected by the Sponsorship Council. These Corporate Members were also voting members of the Board of Trustees. In part, the change was precipitated by the merger of all Mercy communities into one single Institute, thereby changing Mercy representation from six to one.

In May 2013, Sister Lillian sent a Memorandum to the Sponsorship Council proposing that they "look to the future to ensure that the legacy of the Sisters is honored and the important work they began continues with the same spirit of generosity and competence."[2] After reminding the Sponsor Council that Mercy Housing was not bound to any canonical requirements, she proposed three possible governance models be considered for Mercy Housing in the future. The goal of any new model was clearly articulated:

- Ensure the vision, mission and values of the Co-Sponsors endure in this ministry when there are no longer any Sisters involved in the governance of Mercy Housing.

- Clarify the role of the MHI Board and staff in assuring Catholic Heritage.

- Facilitate an orderly transition to lay leadership in the future.[3]

The models proposed for consideration were Public Juridic Person, Private Juridic Person, and Civil Law Status with Catholic Heritage. As objectively as she could, Sister Lillian explained the implications of each model and supplied questions for reflection. The Public Juridic Person model was already being used by some Catholic hospital systems like Catholic Health Initiatives. That model meant that property would be considered as ecclesiastical goods, and rights of ownership and administration would be subject to Canon Law. It would also mean that the organization would be considered as representative of the Catholic Church. Such things as the sale of property in excess of stated amounts would need Church approval. In civil law, the PJP has no recognition or status.

The second model proposed for study was the Private Juridic Person. This model would identify Mercy Housing as the work of Catholics but not a Catholic work.

Since properties are not ecclesiastical goods, no permissions would be involved in their sale, development, or demolition. The Competent Authority, in this case the Church, retained oversight but it was unclear what that really meant.

The final model was Civil Law Status with Catholic Heritage. This model would eliminate both the Sponsor Council and the Corporate Member Group and vest all decision rights in the Board of Trustees. The Board would be self-perpetuating and not subject to Canon Law or Church authority. Care was taken to ensure that the vision and legacy of the founders, Catholic values, and Catholic Social Teaching would be preserved.

For seven years, the sponsors weighed the options to determine what might work best in the future. By December 2020, the decision was made to adopt the model of Civil Law Status with Catholic Heritage. A "Coming to Completion Ceremony, Mercy Housing Corporate Member Group" ritual was held that December. In the ritual, Ismael Guerrero, Chief Executive Officer of Mercy Housing, made the following commitment:

> We promise to fulfill the Vision, Mission, and Core Values through impactful, meaningful work. We promise to make choices to lead by example and embody the values of the Women Religious who founded and sustained Mercy Housing.[4]

Specifically, Mercy Housing leadership was asked: "Will you follow the legacy of the Sisters as inspiration, hope, and a source of mercy to govern and lead the organization?"[5] Patricia Cochran, speaking for the Board of Trustees, and Ismael Guerreo, speaking for the Mercy Housing staff, gave a resounding: "We will." Mercy Housing was now a Legacy Ministry, but what does that mean in practice?

Over the past 40 years, actions, not just words, have shown what Mercy Housing values and what it strives to embody. It is seen in the choices that were made, the challenges that were embraced, and the courage and dedication with which the whole organization, from top to bottom, has lived that legacy day after day. As a result of that witness, it is possible to identify seven principles that guide the path of the ministry into the future.

- It is always about people.

- Balancing Mission and Margin is essential.

- It is core to the ministry to exercise the courage to do the right thing.

- It is Better Together; relationships and community are vital to success.

- Empowerment of the Served is critical to a person's successful transition from being unsheltered to permanent housing.

- Leaders must be adept at Reading the Signs of the Times.

- Flexibility, creativity, perseverance and adaptability are building blocks of the ministry.

When these seven principles are alive and central to the ministry, then it is being faithful to the commitment to be a "legacy" ministry. So, what does that look like?

It is always about people.

In reflecting on the history of Mercy Housing, it is immediately apparent that persons in need prompted its creation. Evictions, children at risk, the overall health impact of being unsheltered, the urgency of housing stability for sustaining dignity of life, and other such realities challenged the religious founders to do something to make a difference. It was about providing a pathway to a better life. Maintaining the status quo was not an option because the absence of an acceptable level of housing undermined human dignity. This urgency was articulated in the United States

Conference of Bishops statement, "The Right to a Decent Home," which supported the sisters' commitment to the housing ministry.

> Addressing ourselves to our own people and to the whole country, we plead with all, in both the private and the public sector, to confront our housing crisis with the courage, conviction, and talent that have brought about our greatest achievements in the past.

> … We cannot deny the crying need for decent housing experienced by the least of the brethren in our society. Effective love of neighbor involves concern for his or her living conditions.[6]

An example of this focus on people is found in the establishment of Mercy Housing Northwest. The six founding religious communities came together because they were impelled to address the needs of children at risk due to either substandard or no housing.

The founding religious communities saw housing as essential for the well-being of children. Many of the sisters who became early property managers were educators who understood the impact of such housing on children. With cramped surroundings, sometimes limited lighting, noisy environments, and little heat, children were not able to thrive. Some dropped out of school or became trapped in a myth that they were of no value and would never be able to better their situation. Sister Jane Gerety RSM, a Mercy Housing Board member, expresses the conviction of Mercy Housing's founders when she says: "I don't think you can have good education or healthcare without decent affordable housing."[7]

What the early leaders discovered was that people needed help to be able to sustain affordable housing. It was one thing to provide a place to call home but helping people to sustain housing was another. Many residents lacked basic skills in budgeting, nutrition, or parenting. That realization led to the establishment of Mercy Housing Management Group. The needs of those served always act as the lens through which decisions are made. Sister Jane Gerety notes that it is never just about buildings. "Buildings are important but what is more important is the community of residents within the building. For people to thrive there has to be a caring community."[8]

Balancing Mission and Margin is essential.

Some understandings grow out of lived experience. Initially the movement was to address urgent needs. Not a lot of study was given to long-term consequences. Over time it proved true that not every opportunity was a good opportunity. Even though the project might tug at the heart, it was not necessarily workable in the long run. The cost of upkeep, funding the debt, and refinancing when tax credits expired all had to be factored into determining the viability of moving forward with the project or not.

Recognizing the need for centralizing markets and transferring some properties to other holders was painful, but it was the only way in which the margin (funding) could sustain the mission. Mercy Housing had to learn that it couldn't do everything but if financially healthy, it could take on projects which were risky and challenging. What had to be examined was how that project would respond to mission imperatives without jeopardizing the ongoing stability of Mercy Housing as a whole. That was what the "Transformation" was all about. Without such a profound reordering, Mercy Housing would not have been able to weather the major tempests of the Great Recession in 2007.

The founding communities were keenly aware of the challenges involved in balancing mission and margin. They encouraged Trustees and Mercy Housing Leadership:

> To consider both short-term and long-term trends and goals in your planning efforts. Doing very well what we do today, coupled with envisioning new possibilities for extending our work leads to good stewardship of the resources entrusted to us and helps to build a more just society where all are welcome and able to achieve their dreams.[9]

It is core to the ministry to exercise the courage to do the right thing.

The field of affordable housing is not easy. Those who work in the field as developers, property managers, resident service staff, or leaders are sustained by a passion for justice and the fire of compassion. Without those two elements, people would quickly burn out and leave the field. It takes enormous courage to face the challenges that are part of every project. It takes courage for developers to face hostile city officials or participate in public hearings when opposition to projects is strong. Hostility is hard to take when you know the need is critical and urgent.

Courage is needed in other ways as well. There is always the risk of failure, either because coalitions collapse, natural disasters occur, unpredictable construction issues arise, or funding sources withdraw. When such failures occur, not only is the pre-development investment lost, but there is also the potential of the failure causing damage to Mercy Housing's reputation. That is why the Sunnydale housing project in San Francisco was so risky. The circumstances were so dire that the possibility of not succeeding loomed large. People who lived in the area saw no way out but death.[10] Jane Graf felt that it was risky but also the most profound work that Mercy Housing could do. As she said at the time: "For those who suggested it was too risky, my reply was 'that is why we must do this.'"[11]

It is Better Together. Relationships and Community are vital to success.

The two principles, it is better together and relationships and community are vital to success, cannot really be separated. They link together. From the very beginning of Mercy Housing's ministry, its founders reached out to others of like vision and heart for support. They recognized that they could not succeed in their mission if they did not have collaborators to supply what they lacked. The inclusion of Jim Tomlinson in creating the shape of the ministry is testimony to that conviction.

In the pamphlet "Mercy Housing's Guiding Values" is found the following statement: "Mercy Housing's history is one of collaboration and interfaith partnership, to work with all people and organizations to make a difference in communities.[12] At first the collaborative efforts of the ministry focused on investors and funders, but that would soon change when Sister Lillian Murphy became CEO in 1986. Sister Lillian invited other religious communities to join with Mercy Housing's efforts to provide affordable housing for families and seniors. Eventually 13 religious communities joined together as co-sponsors. That was only one aspect of collaboration. There were more.

Mercy Community Capital is a vivid example of Mercy Housing's priority of collaboration. In 1983, Mercy Housing took steps to assist other affordable housing providers who needed help. Mercy Community Capital was established to provide affordable housing financing where conventional financing is unavailable or hard to obtain. It also focuses on lending monies through peer Community Development Financial institutions to expand its impact. "Rather than competing with other CDFIs, MCC emphasizes collaborative marketing and co-lending to leverage market-specific expertise and scarce capital resources, especially when a developer's financing needs exceeds a single CDFI's loan limit."[13] Over $3 billion has been leveraged in development costs for affordable housing properties through this process.

The early leaders of Mercy Housing were sisters who had experience as hospital administrators. They had seen first-hand the link between health and housing. For them, it was a natural fit to work together with healthcare systems. That collaborative linkage took the form of Strategic Healthcare Partners. Once more, the shared approach to addressing the housing crisis resulted in new opportunities and increased resources flowing into Mercy Housing.

The success of Mercy Housing brought in more collaborative partners. Existing housing agencies that needed partners or needed to turn their holdings over to a larger entity sought out Mercy Housing as the collaborator of choice. That is how Mercy Housing Northwest came to be and how the Wheaton Franciscan portfolio became part of Mercy's property. Partners didn't need to be Catholic. Those who had a shared vision and embraced shared values were welcome to join in the work.

The dynamic of co-sponsorship and that of Strategic Healthcare Partners involved large collaborations, but smaller, personal linkages are equally as important. Building relationships with both funders and the civic community is crucial in the development process. To be successful, you have to have a well-developed network of support and advocacy to move projects forward. Steve Spears points out that developments are just one phone call from collapse if a funding agency loses trust in Mercy Housing leadership.[14]

Transparency with all involved — funders, partners, neighbors, and civic leaders — is essential in acquiring that trust.

Only when trust is established can you decrease the fears that sometimes surround the impact of new affordable housing on a neighborhood. That trust necessitates conversations, availability, and a genuine desire to help the neighborhood achieve its goals. Projects like Savannah Gardens highlight how important the task of building relationships is. When successful, all participants feel ownership of the project and can echo the words of Edna Jackson, former mayor of Savannah, when she says: "We were a team. We worked together. We made decisions together."[15]

As Mercy Housing leadership gained experience, there was a widening of its vision. The fostering of community, which was part of the vision from the start, initially focused on building community among residents within the development. With time, that focus expanded to look at the needs of the neighborhoods in which those developments were located. Developments like those of Sunnydale in San Francisco and Heritage Place and Heritage Corner & Row apartments in Savannah are examples of that broader vision.

Empowerment of the Served is critical to a person's successful transition from being unsheltered to permanent housing.

When Sister Terese Tracy first recruited members of the Omaha Mercy community to become part of Mercy Housing, she outlined values and practices that would be essential. Property managers had to understand the aspects of tending the properties, but first and foremost they were to embrace values like empowerment, human dignity, mutual participation, and justice. Property managers were to be more than caretakers of buildings. They were responsible for fostering the growth and development of vital communities. Supportive services and programs were highlighted as a core element. The goal was to empower the residents to control their own environment and gain skills in decision-making, as well as those skills needed for sustaining their housing.[16] People skills were critical for the success of the mission.

That pattern of putting people first has been core to Mercy Housing's mission over the last 40 years. Patricia Cochran, former Board Chair of Mercy Housing, points out that "Resident Services are our North Star."[17] Without such supportive services, it would become just another housing provider rather than the transforming agent it is. When Sister Jeanne Warde started out as a property manager, she discovered there were not enough hours in the day to meet all the needs of her residents. One of her major tasks was to foster among the residents a community of caring where they learned to trust and depend upon each other. No property manager or resident service personnel can be available to everyone at every hour of the day. It takes the whole residential community to make that happen.

Addressing a common concern was part of the learnings needed by residents at Folsom Terrace in Folsom, California. A family development with many children, residents were gravely concerned about the speed of traffic on Duchow Way, the street directly in front of their apartments. Mercy's Property Management staff helped the residents learn how to approach local civic leaders to advocate for speed bumps. From beginning to end, the process belonged to the residents who gained the skills and confidence to present their petition to the city council. They were successful. They had taken control of their neighborhood and had learned they could bring about change.

There is no one pattern of support that fits every situation. In Mercy Housing's developments for veterans, accommodation to disabilities must be considered, as well as the emotional wounds that are brought home after war. Helping residents reintegrate into society is critical. According to the RAND Corporation, a think tank focused on research and development for the armed services, approximately one-third of the 1.6 million returning veterans from the conflicts in Iraq and Afghanistan will have returned with traumatic brain injury, PTSD, and/or severe depression.[18] Mercy Housing's supportive services are an essential component in their recovery journey.

Not all residents need such intensive assistance. Many are working single parents who cannot afford full rental costs. One unexpected crisis puts them a step away from homelessness. Liliana, a young mother, is such an example. Her daughter was born with cerebral palsy and hypoplastic left heart syndrome. Liliana knew that she had to find a safe place for her daughter, one that she could afford. That was when someone connected her with Mercy Housing. When Liliana came to Mercy Housing, she found an affordable place to live but also a network of supportive services that allowed her to follow her dream of becoming a nurse and eventually buying her own home.[19]

For family housing properties, a combination of after-school programming and computer labs help children succeed in school as well as allowing parents to work, knowing their children are safe and well cared for. Senior residents also have special needs, especially for connection, safety, and community. The benefits of partnering with Strategic Healthcare Partners means that wellness programs and normal healthcare screenings can be part of the supportive services brought into the facility for its residents. Boulevard Court in Sacramento is an example of such a facility. Among the services it offers its residents are:

- Resident Services provided by Mercy Housing, The Effort and Turning Point Community Programs

- Community building with meeting rooms, kitchen, and bathrooms
- Computer room
- Lounge
- Laundry room
- Counselling offices
- Federal Qualified Heath Center run by The Effort[20]

In exploring all the diversity and opportunities offered by Mercy Housing's Resident Services, one is struck by its practicality and creativity. You can find cooking classes, nutrition classes, book clubs, wellness programs, sobriety programs, or community gardens. Each property's offerings are shaped and reshaped by resident input as well as resident talent. It is the actualization of what is said in "Reflections on the Future of the Mercy Housing Ministry" — "The resident programs at Mercy Housing are not an after-thought they are our first thought."[21]

Leaders must be adept at Reading the Signs of the Times.

Throughout the history of Mercy Housing, leaders have had to read the signs of the time, whether that meant understanding the ever-changing financial world or the urgent needs of its residents. To safeguard the stability of the ministry, it was necessary to understand the market in which it functioned and read the emergent needs and trends that would impact that market. Since developments sometimes take between six to ten years to move from conception to fulfillment, it is not enough to just know today's realities.

Reading political trends is also a major challenge. Since funding is often tied to governmental programs or things like tax credits, it is vital to be able to project ahead on their impact on both development and resident services costs. This is especially true when governmental mandates are not funded fully.

Sometimes, however, reading the signs of the times can lead to tough choices. That is what happened when Mercy Housing Leadership had to turn over to other affordable housing providers properties that were too widespread to be adequately managed. To some it seemed like a betrayal of Mercy Housing's commitment to those who were poor, but such a choice was necessary to be able to sustain the mission over time.

Reading the inner spirit of the ministry itself is also critical in maintaining vibrancy of mission. Understanding when encouragement is needed or what challenge might be required is part of that "spirit reading." The Mercy Housing Board did that when it elected to use part of monies awarded to Mercy Housing by the Yield Giving Foundation, for making a significant difference in the lives of those served, to reward the employees who made such a distinction possible. This action was faithful to the sponsors' request that Mercy Housing staff take care of each other:

> Mercy Housing boards and staff spend many hours caring for those who need some of the basic necessities of human life. This work can be very draining and you need to take care of yourselves and each other. Take time to celebrate current and past success and express appreciation for all those who have contributed to that success.[22]

Flexibility, creativity, perseverance, and adaptability are building blocks of the ministry.

Sister Jane Gerety reminds us that these "four elements have been hallmarks of Mercy Housing since its very beginning."[23] The first sister property managers and developers just had to figure things out using their creativity, spirit of adventure, and, most of all, perseverance. When projects addressing urgent needs take years to complete because of local or state regulation, or opposition from neighbors, lots of patience is needed. Only keeping the goal in sight makes that possible.

The founding sisters trusted their instincts when things did not seem to be consistent with what was needed to honor human dignity, or when it failed to respect the needs of residents. It took courage from them to break the link with DBSI, their investment partner, because values didn't match. The courage for such action was rooted in the conviction that words must match deeds. Mercy Housing had to be what it said it was, true to its mission:

> To create stable, vibrant, healthy communities by developing and operating quality, affordable, service-enriched housing for individuals, families, seniors and those with special needs who lack the economic resources to access safe affordable housing opportunities.[24]

As Mercy Housing worked on the preservation of aging housing or historical preservation projects, developers had to consistently adapt to what they discovered. Creative ways around what might seem insurmountable were the order of the day. The characteristics weren't outlined in a manual. They were made evident in action.

A Legacy Ministry

In 2017, when the religious community founders recognized that changes in the circumstances of religious life today meant that fewer sisters would be available to serve on corporate boards, responsibilities shifted to lay partners. The sisters knew the ministry would be in good hands as it became a legacy ministry with a self-perpetuating board in 2021. As they reflected on the future of the ministry, they captured their reflections in "Reflections on the Future of the Mercy Housing Ministry." A powerful document, it painted the vision of what could be and what must be treasured. They said to leadership, board members, and the organization as a whole:

> We are handing on to you a precious ministry that we believe in and have nurtured since its founding, just as the Wheaton Franciscan Sisters handed on to Mercy Housing their cherished housing ministry for safe keeping. We ask that you remain faithful to the Vision, Mission, Core Values and Operating Commitments that have focused the work of a tremendously talented and compassionate staff. We encourage you to reflect on these statements often. As faithful Trustees, please continue to use these documents and the spirit they have inspired to direct this ministry[25]

Mercy Housing leadership strives to respond to that request through its fidelity to the mission. Speaking as a current board member, Sister Jane Gerety affirms that commitment: "Today, Mercy Housing continues to live out the legacy of the thirteen women's religious communities who offered crucial support for the great work of providing safe, affordable housing so that so many could thrive."[26] In looking to the future, Patricia Cochran, former Board Chair, hopes that the ministry will continue to grow the number of residents served and the properties in which they are housed. She notes that it isn't just a question of having housing, but it is also about the quality of life fostered within those properties.

One of the critical things to remember in Patricia's perception is that Mercy Housing is not only a real estate business. It is a ministry to the most vulnerable. That is why it exists.[27] Ismael Guerrero sums up this moment of Mercy Housing history:

"Our commitment to the dignity and well-being of those most in need remains the cornerstone of our work. Together, we are not just building homes but creating communities where hope, opportunity, and resilience can flourish."[28]

At the heart of that hope is the challenge of passing on to the next generation of Mercy Housing leaders, to every member of the organization, the values and vision of the legacy received. The energies and guidance from Mercy Housing's story supports present efforts and illumines the path to be followed. It is not a story solely of the past. It is a living story that continues to transform the lives of the most vulnerable. Patricia Cochran reflects that passing on the values and vision of the founding sisters is a critical task. "The passion for serving the most vulnerable is fed by the commitment to provide the services that empower residents to succeed. It is in recognizing that you have not just answered a need — you have transformed lives!"[29]

For Your Reflection and Conversation

- The author of this work identifies seven principles which characterize Mercy Housing's activities. Have you found this to be true to your experience of the ministry? What three principles do you feel are most important?

- Mercy Housing is deemed a "legacy" ministry, meaning that it will continue to live out the mission and values of its founders. What does that legacy mean to you and what do you personally need to actively foster it continuation?

APPENDIX A

MERCY HOUSING PROPERTIES
AS OF DECEMBER 2024

Alabama

Arbors at Ellington	Pleasant Grove	AL

Arizona

Avondale Senior Housing	Avondale	AZ
Camelot Casitas	Phoenix	AZ
Casa De Merced	Tolleson	AZ
Casa De Shanti	Phoenix	AZ
El Mirage Senior Village	El Mirage	AZ
Guadalupe – Nuestro Pueblito	Guadalupe	AZ
Lemon Grove Apartments	Phoenix	AZ
Mesa Senior Meadows	Mesa	AZ
Page Commons	Gilbert	AZ
Peoria Place	Phoenix	AZ
Plazas de Merced	Phoenix	AZ
The Casalote (under construction)	Phoenix	AZ
Vista Allegre	Glendale	AZ
Western Winds Apt	Tucson	AZ

California

10th and Mission Family Housing	San Francisco	CA
1028 Howard Street	San Francisco	CA
1100 Ocean Avenue	San Francisco	CA
1101 Howard Street	San Francisco	CA
111 Jones Street	San Francisco	CA
1180 4th Street	San Francisco	CA
1633 Valencia (under construction)	San Francisco	CA
1801 West Capitol	West Sacramento	CA
1880 Pine	San Francisco	CA
205 Jones Street	San Francisco	CA

2098 California (under construction)	San Francisco	CA
290 Melosi	San Francisco	CA
300 Alamitos Senior Housing (under construction)	Long Beach	CA
345 Arguello	San Francisco	CA
3552 Whittier	Los Angeles	CA
455 Fell	San Francisco	CA
600 7th	San Francisco	CA
6th Street Place	Los Angeles	CA
7th and H	Sacramento	CA
95 Laguna	San Francisco	CA
All Hallows Community	San Francisco	CA
Ardenaire Apartments	Sacramento	CA
Baldwin Rose Apartments	El Monte	CA
Bayview Hill Gardens	San Francisco	CA
Bear Mountain Residences	San Andreas	CA
Bennett House	Fairfax	CA
Beverly Terrace	Marysville	CA
Bill Sorro Community	San Francisco	CA
Boulevard Court	Sacramento	CA
Brentwood Green Valley Apts.	Brentwood	CA
Britton Court	San Francisco	CA
Burbank Boulevard Senior	Los Angeles	CA
Camino Alto	Mill Valley	CA
Cantebria Senior Homes	Encinitas	CA
Caroline Severance Manor	Los Angeles	CA
Carter Terrace	San Francisco	CA
Casa Alegre	Anaheim	CA
Casa de la Mission	San Francisco	CA
Casa Merced,	Oxnard	CA
Casa San Juan	Oxnard	CA
Casa Verde	San Leandro	CA
Casala	San Francisco	CA
Coastside	Half Moon Bay	CA
Colma Veterans Village	Colma	CA

Colonia San Martin	Sacramento	CA
Columbia Park	Sacramento	CA
Countrywood Apartments	Marysville	CA
Creekview Manor	Folsom	CA
Crossroad Gardens	Sacramento	CA
Cypress Lane Family (under construction)	Paradise	CA
Derek Silva Community	San Francisco	CA
Diamond Sunrise	Diamond Springs	CA
Diamond Sunrise II	Diamond Springs	CA
Dorothy Day	San Francisco	CA
Downtown Villas	Santa Cruz	CA
East Leland Court	Pittsberg	CA
Eden House	San Leandro	CA
Edith Witt Senior Community	San Francisco	CA
El Centro Residential	Santa Cruz	CA
El Dorado Haven (under construction)	El Dorado	CA
El Monte Veterans Village	El Monte	CA
Esparto Family Apartments	Esparto	CA
Esperanza Crossing	Esparto	CA
Folsom Gardens I	Folsom	CA
Folsom Gardens II	Folsom	CA
Francis of Assisi	San Francisco	CA
Garden Park Apartment Community	Pleasant Hill	CA
Gault Street Senior	Santa Cruz	CA
Gleason Park Apartments	Stockton	CA
Grand and Venice	Los Angeles	CA
Grizzly Hollow	Gault	CA
Hacienda Heights	Richmond	CA
Hamilton Apartments	Oakland	CA
Heritage Gardens	Long Beach	CA
Heritage Homes	San Francisco	CA
Historic Live Oak - Odd Fellows	Live Oak	CA
Howard and Irene Levine Senior Community	Los Angeles	CA
Hunters Point Shipyard Block		

(under construction)	San Francisco	CA
Jefferson Park Terrace	Los Angeles	CA
JFK Towers	San Francisco	CA
John King Sr	San Francisco	CA
Junipero Serra	San Francisco	CA
Kennedy Estates	Sacramento	CA
Kent Garden Senior Housing	San Lorenzo	CA
Kimball Tower	National City	CA
La Mancha Way Apartments	Sacramento	CA
Lagoon Beach Cooperative	Santa Cruz	CA
Lance Apartments	Carmichael	CA
Land Park Woods	Sacramento	CA
Linbrook Court	Anaheim	CA
Lohse Apartments	Roseville	CA
Manzanita	San Leandro	CA
Maria B Freitas	San Rafael	CA
Marlton Manor	San Francisco	CA
Martin Luther King Village	Sacramento	CA
Martinelli	San Rafael	CA
Mather Veterans Village	Rancho Cordova	CA
Mather Veterans Village Phase 3	Sacramento	CA
McAuley Meadows	Auburn	CA
Meadows 1 Apartments (managed only)	Jackson	CA
Mercy Family Plaza	San Francisco	CA
Mercy Gardens	San Diego	CA
Mercy Oaks Village	Redding	CA
Mercy Riverside	Red Bluff	CA
Mercy Terrace	San Francisco	CA
Mercy Village Folsom	Folsom	CA
Middlefield Junction (under construction)	Redwood City	CA
Mission Creek Senior	San Francisco	CA
Monsignor Lyne	San Francisco	CA
Montclair and Tolton Court	Los Angeles	CA
Morgan Tower	National City	CA
Natalie Gubb Commons I and II	San Francisco	CA

Neary Lagoon Apartments	Santa Cruz	CA
New Dana Strand	Los Angeles	CA
North Auburn at Rock Creek	Auburn	CA
Notre Dame Senior Housing	San Francisco	CA
Nueva Vista	Santa Cruz	CA
Oceana Terrace	Pacifica	CA
Osocales	Soquel	CA
Padre Apartments	San Francisco	CA
Padre Palou	San Francisco	CA
Park Terrace	Yuba City	CA
Pinewood Court	Williams	CA
Placentia Veterans Village	Placentia	CA
Plaza Maria	San Jose	CA
Polk Street Senior Community	San Francisco	CA
Presentation Senior Community	San Francisco	CA
Quinn Cottages	Sacramento	CA
Richmond Hills	San Francisco	CA
Riverview Homes	Truckee	CA
Russell Manor	Sacramento	CA
San Felipe	Los Angeles	CA
Santana Apartments	Oakland	CA
Schoolhouse Station Vista Grande	Daly City	CA
Serna Village	McClellan	CA
Sister Lillian Murphy Senior Community	San Francisco	CA
St Andrews Senior Housing	Daly City	CA
St Claire at Capitol Park	Sacramento	CA
St Francis Terrace	Sacramento	CA
St Mary's Tower	Long Beach	CA
Star View Court	San Francisco	CA
Sunset Valley	Wheatland	CA
Sycamore – La Playa	Santa Cruz	CA
Tahanen	San Francisco	CA
Tahoe Valley Townhomes	South Lake Tahoe	CA
The Acacia (under construction)	Palo Alto	CA
The Arbor at Hesperian	San Lorenzo	CA

The Arc Mercy	San Francisco	CA
The Arlington	San Francisco	CA
The Courtyards on Orange Grove	North Highlands	CA
The Dudley	San Francisco	CA
The Hamilton Rehab (under construction)	Oakland	CA
The Heights on Stockton	Sacramento	CA
The Kelsey Civic Center (under construction)	San Francisco	CA
The Madonna	San Francisco	CA
The Open House Community at 55 Laguna	San Francisco	CA
The Rose	San Francisco	CA
The Vineyard Townhomes	Anaheim	CA
Tierra Del Sol	Cathedral City	CA
Trailside Terrace	Shingle Springs	CA
Vera Haile Senior Housing	San Francisco	CA
Villa Amador	Brentwood	CA
Villa Columba	Red Bluff	CA
Villa de Vida	Poway	CA
Villa Madera	Oxnard	CA
Villa St Joseph	Orange	CA
Village Park Apartments	Sacramento	CA
Washington Street CO-OP	Santa Cruz	CA
West Beamer Place	Woodland	CA
Westbrook Plaza	San Francisco	CA
White Rock Village	Eldorado Hills	CA

Colorado

901 Navajo (under construction)	Denver	CO
Bluff Lake Apartments	Denver	CO
Clare Gardens	Denver	CO
Clare of Assisi Homes	Westminster	CO
Dayspring Villa	Denver	CO
Decatur Place Apts	Denver	CO
Francis Heights	Denver	CO

Franconia	Denver	CO
Grace Apartments Re-Syndication	Denver	CO
Holly Park	Commerce City	CO
Merced De Las Animas	Durango	CO
Northfield Commons	Ft. Collins	CO
Parkside Apartments	Denver	CO
Pinon Terrace	Durango	CO
Springfield Court	Fort Collins	CO
The Aromor	Denver	CO
The Rose on Colfax	Denver	CO
Valle De Merced	Durango	CO
Villa Maria	Westminster	CO
Willow Street Apartments	Denver	CO

Georgia

Adamsville Green	Atlanta	GA
Allegre Point Senior Resident	Decatur	GA
Antioch Gardens and Villas	Stone Mountain	GA
Chamblee Senior Apartments	Chamblee	GA
Etowah Terrace	Rome	GA
Henderson Place (under construction)	Atlanta	GA
Heritage Corner and Heritage Row	Savannah	GA
Heritage Place	Savannah	GA
Magnolia Village	Americus	GA
Mercy Park Chamblee	Chamblee	GA
Orchard Grove	Madison	GA
Renaissance at Park Place South	Atlanta	GA
Reynoldstown	Atlanta	GA
Savannah Gardens	Savannah	GA
Savannah Gardens III	Savannah	GA
Savannah Gardens IV	Savannah	GA
Savannah Gardens V	Savannah	GA
Savannah Gardens VI	Savannah	GA
Savannah Gardens Senior Residence	Savannah	GA
Terraces at Parkview	Lithonia	GA
The Atrium at College Town	Atlanta	GA

| The Rose of Sharon Apartments | Savannah | GA |
| Thrive Sweet Auburn | Atlanta | GA |

Idaho

12th And River Senior Apartments	Boise	ID
Eagle Senior Village	Eagle	ID
Hawthorne Village	Moscow	ID
Independence Hill	Moscow	ID
Sisters Villa	Eagle	ID

Illinois

850 Eastwood	Chicago	IL
Assisi Homes of Gurnee	Gurnee	IL
Batavia Apartments	Batavia	IL
Belray Apartments	Chicago	IL
Cannon Place	Danville	IL
Canticle Place	Wheaton	IL
Carlton Apartments	Chicago	IL
Colony Park	Carol Stream	IL
Constitution House	Aurora	IL
Countryside Seniors Apartments	Countryside	IL
Delmar Apartments	Chicago	IL
Englewood	Chicago	IL
Grayslake Senior Housing	Grayslake	IL
Harold Washington Apts	Chicago	IL
Holland Apartments	Chicago	IL
LaSalle Manor	LaSalle	IL
Major Jenkins	Chicago	IL
Malden Arms II Apartments	Chicago	IL
Marian Park	Wheaton	IL
Miriam Apartments	Chicago	IL
Pullman Wheelworks	Chicago	IL
River Station Senior	Kankakee	IL
River West Commons	Elgin	IL
Roseland Place	Chicago	IL
Roseland Village	Chicago	IL

Schiff Residences	Chicago	IL
South Loop Apartments	Chicago	IL
The Lofts on Arthington	Chicago	IL
The Studios (managed only)	Chicago	IL
Wentworth Commons	Chicago	IL

Indiana

Alexandria Manor	Alexandria	IN
Cedar Commons	Indianapolis	IN
Spruce Manor	Indianapolis	IN

Iowa

Sherwood Place	Council Bluffs	IA

Kansas

Cedar Park Place (managed only)	Great Bend	KS

Kentucky

Dublin Manor	Paducah	KY
Lone Oak Manor	Paducah	KY
McAuley Manor	Paducah	KY
Mercy Manor	Paducah	KY
Princeton Manor	Princeton	KY
Sacred Heart Village I	Louisville	KY
Sacred Heart Village II	Louisville	KY
Sacred Heart Village III	Louisville	KY

Missouri

Mercy Village Joplin	Joplin	MO

Nebraska

Crestview Village	La Vista	NE
Falgrove Apartments	Omaha	NE
Timbercreek	Omaha	NE
Mercy House	Omaha	NE
Mercy Northglen	Lincoln	NE
Western Manor	Lincoln	NE

North Carolina

Mercy Place - Belmont	Belmont	NC

Ohio

Charles Crest I	Rossford	OH
Charles Crest II	Oregon	OH
Charles Meadows	Tiffin	OH
Siena Springs I	Dayton	OH
Siena Springs II	Dayton	OH
St. Theresa Village	Cincinnati	OH

Oregon

Berry Ranch (under construction)	Portland	OR
Mercy Greenbrae at Marylhurst Commons	Lake Oswego	OR

South Carolina

Marshside Village	North Charleston	SC
Mulberry Court Apartments	Greenville	SC
Olii Place	Mauldin	SC

South Dakota

Driftwood Estates	Rapid City	SD
Northern Heights	Rapid City	SD

Tennessee

St. Marys Riverview I	Knoxville	TN
St. Marys Riverview II	Knoxville	TN
St. Marys Villa	Knoxville	TN

Utah

Francis Peak View	Kaysville	UT

Washington

Allegre Villa	Winlock	WA
Angle Lake (under construction)	Seatac	WA
Appian Way	Kent	WA
Aviva Crossing (under construction)	Tacoma	WA
Boundary Village	Blaine	WA
Cambridge Apartments	Centralia	WA

Cascade Apartments	Granite Falls	WA
Catalina Apartments	Tacoma	WA
Cedarwood I	Lake Stevens	WA
Cedarwood IV	Lake Stevens	WA
Columbia City Station	Seattle	WA
Columbia Heights Apartments	Vancouver	WA
Eleanor Apartments	Bellingham	WA
Eliza McCabe Townhomes	Tacoma	WA
Emerald City Commons	Seattle	WA
Evergreen Manor	Concrete	WA
Evergreen Ridge	Bellingham	WA
Evergreen Vista	Olympia	WA
Evergreen Vista II	Olympia	WA
Family Tree	Everett	WA
Ferndale Square	Ferndale	WA
Ferndale Villa	Ferndale	WA
Fircrest	Mt. Vernon	WA
Gardner House	Seattle	WA
Hillside Gardens	Tacoma	WA
Lake Stevens Manor	Lake Stevens	WA
Lake Village East	Lake Stevens	WA
Lincoln Way	Lynnwood	WA
Lincoln Way II	Lynwood	WA
Mercy Magnuson Place South	Seattle	WA
Mercy Magnuson Place North	Seattle	WA
Mercy Rosa Franklin Place	Tacoma	WA
Millworks Family Housing	Bellingham	WA
Monroe Villa	Monroe	WA
New Tacoma	Tacoma	WA
New Tacoma Senior Phase II	Tacoma	WA
Olympic Apartments	Mt. Vernon	WA
Othello East	Seattle	WA
Othello West	Seattle	WA
Pilchuck	Marysville	WA
Sandstone	Tenino	WA
Skagit Village	Mt. Vernon	WA

Sterling Meadows	Bellingham	WA
Sterling Senior Housing	Bellingham	WA
Tahoma View	Tacoma	WA
Trailview	Bellingham	WA
Villa Kathleen	Burlington	WA
Woodlake Manor	Snohomish	WA

Wisconsin

Assisi Homes of Kenosha	Kenosha	WI
Assisi Homes of Neenah	Neenah	WI
Greenwich Park Apartments	Milwaukee	WI
Jefferson Court Apartments	Milwaukee	WI
Johnston Center Residences	Milwaukee	WI
Marian Housing Center	Racine	WI
McAuley Apartments	Milwaukee	WI
Saxony Manor	Kenosha	WI

ENDNOTES

Introduction

[1]   Ismael Guerrero, Community Matters newsletter, 2024.

[2]   Mercy Housing Website blog, The Dignity, Love and Warmth of Home, 1-2-2024.

[3]   Letter from Ismael Guerrero to Sr. Katherine Doyle RSM, 2-3-2025.

Chapter 1

[1]   Interview with Patricia O'Roark, 12-7-23.

[2]   Charism is a gift of the Holy Spirit to a person or group for the benefit of others. The charism of a religious community is the spirit of that group which shapes the way they give their lives for others and any spirit qualities of heart which they embody.

[3]   Bourke, M. Carmel, *A Woman Sings of Mercy: Reflections on the Life and Spirit of Mother Catherine McAuley Foundress of the Sisters of Mercy.* (Alexandria, Australia: E. J. Dwyer, 1987), p.8.

[4]   Sullivan, Mary C., *Path of Mercy, the Life of Catherine McAuley,* (Washington, D. C: Catholic University of American Press, 2012), p.55.

[5]   Kozol, Jonathan, *Rachel and Her Children, Homeless Families in America*, (New York: Three Rivers Press, 1988), p.6.

[6]   Ibid., p.9

[7]   Sullivan, *Path of Mercy*, p.45.

[8]   Sullivan, *Path of Mercy*, p. 53.

[9]   Sullivan, *Path of Mercy*, pp.55-56.

Chapter 2

[1]   USCCB, *The Right to a Decent Home: A Pastoral Response to the Crisis in Housing*. #1

[2]   USCCB, *The Right to a Decent Home*, #2, #39, #43.

[3]   Wertz. Mary Regina, *Our Beloved Union, A History of the Sisters of Mercy of the Union*. (Westminster, Maryland: Christian Classics, 1989), p.66.

[4]   Wertz, *Our Beloved Union*. p.74.

[5]   A Chapter is an official gathering of a community, usually with representative members elected by the whole, which is empowered by the Constitution of the congregation to make policy and corporate decisions. It is the highest governing locus in a religious congregation.

[6]   Betty Barrett, RSM, quoted in Wertz, p.74.

[7]   Interview with Catherine Kuper, 10-31-23.

[8]   Letter of Sister Betty Barrett. Quoted in Wertz, p.74.

[9]   Wertz, p.188.

[10] Interview with Patricia O'Roark, 12/11/2023.

[11] Interview with Patricia O'Roark, 11/13/2023.

[12] Ibid.

[13] Sisters of Mercy, 1980 Omaha Provincial Chapter minutes.

[14] Kuper RSM. 10/31/2023.

[15] Interview with Patricia O'Roark, 12/7/23.

[16] Interview with Rita Parks RSM, 11/13.2023.

[17] Transcript of Interview with Sister Norita Cooney by Patricia O'Roark, pre-2011.

[18] Mercy Housing Website blog, 40 Years of Leadership – Sister Mary Terese Tracy, 2-23-2022.

[19] Ibid.

[20] Ibid.

[21] Kuper, 10/31/2023.

[22] Ibid.

[23] Interview with Jeanne Ward, 11-7-2023.

[24] Parks, 11-13-2023.

[25] Cooney, prior to 2011.

[26] Mary Terese Tracy, memo 1, October 2, 1981.

[27] BVM indicates membership as in the Sisters of the Blessed Virgin Mary.

[28] Tracy, memo 1, October 2,1981.

[29] Mary Terese Tracy, memo 2, November 6, 1981.

[30] Kozal, p.15.

[31] Ibid.

[32] Tracy, memo November 8, 1981.

[33] Ibid.

[34] Ibid.

Chapter 3

[1] Interview with Patricia O'Roark, 11-13-23.

[2] Interview with James Tomlinson, 12-8-23.

[3] Tracy, Memo, January 1982.

[4] Ibid.

[5] Transcript of interview with Joan Martin 8-7-2007.

[6] Transcript of interview with Jeanne Ward, 8-7-2007,

[7] Interview with Jeanne Ward, 11-7-23.

[8] Ibid.

[9] Ibid.

[10] Ward,8-7-2007.

[11] A novice is new member of a religious community who has not yet made vows. They technically don't become a full member of the congregation until the time of vows.

[12] Interview with Mary Drey, 8-2007.

[13] New York Times, March 8, 1987, Section 8, p.1.

[14] Ibid.

[15] Interview with Jeanne Christensen, 11-10-23.

[16] Ibid.

[17] Ibid.

[18] Ibid.

[19] Ibid.

[20] Ibid.

[21] Transcript, Interview with Joan Marie Martin, undated.

[22] Transcript of interview with Mary Regis Leahy, 4-20-2022.

[23] Leahy, 4-20-2022.

[24] Christensen, 11-10-23.

[25] Leahy, 4-20-2022.

Chapter 4

[1] Mercy Housing Website, Who We Serve.

[2] Interview with Sister Jeanne Christenson, 11-10-2023

[3] Interview with Jim Tomlinson, 12-8-2023

[4]   Mercy Housing Website Blog, 40 Years of Leadership – Founder Patricia O'Roark, 3-26-2024.

[5]   Interview with Sarah Smith, 11-9-2023.

[6]   Website: Mercy Community Capital, https://www.mercyhousing.org/partner-with-us/mercy-community-capital.

[7]   Interview with Sister Mary Regis Leahy, 3-24-22.

[8]   Interview with Sarah Smith, 11- 9-2023.

[9]   Event Log of Mercy Housing Corporation, November 1975-March 1987.

[10]   Mercy Housing, Inc. "Addressing the Housing Crisis", 1988.

[11]   Ibid. p.3.

[12]   Ibid. p.3.

[13]   2001 Annual Report, Mercy Housing System, p.20.

[14]   2020 Mercy Housing Impact Report, p.22.

[15]   Interview with Stefanie Joy, 9- 18-2024.

[16]   Notes from Stefanie Joy, April 14, 2025.

[17]   2001 Annual Report, Mercy Housing System, p.21.

[18]   Interview with Sr. Diane Clyne, 3/6/24.

[19]   News from our Neighborhoods, A Publication of Mercy Housing. Spring 2009, p.17.

[20]   Clyne, 3/6/24.

[21]   News from our Neighborhoods, A Publication of Mercy Housing. Spring 2009, p.17.

[22]   News from our Neighborhoods, A Publication of Mercy Housing. Spring 2009, p.12.

[23]   Letter from Catherine McAuley to Father James Maher, January 10, 1838.

[24]   Transcript of interview with Sr. Gertrude Hoyer CSC, March 3-24-22.

[25]   Ibid.

[26]   Transcript, Hearing of Committee on Financial Services, Subcommittee on Housing and Community Opportunity U.S. House of Representatives, April 25, 2006.

[27]   Hoyer CSC, 3-24-22.

[28]   Interview with Steve Spears, 9-7-24.

[29]   Interview with Colin Morgan-Cross, 8/29/2024.

30 Ibid.

31 Spears, 9-7-24.

32 Ibid.

33 Ibid.

34 Morgan Cross, 8-29-2024.

35 Transcript of interview with Sister Lillian Murphy, March 3-24-22.

36 Letter from Ismael Guerro, 2-3-2025.

Chapter 5
1 Transcript of interview Sr. Richard Mary Burke, 4-20-2022.

2 Transcript of interview with Sisters Norita Cooney and Mary Ellen Quinn, 9- 24-2007.

3 Ibid.

4 Transcript of interview with Sr. Pat Eck, 3-24-2022.

5 Transcript of interview with Sr. Terese Marie Perry, 4-20, 2022,

6 Ibid.

7 Transcript of interview with Sister Maura Power, 4-20-2022.

8 Ibid.

9 Ibid.

10 Eck, 3-24-2022.

11 Von, Hoffman, Alexander." The Transformation of Mercy Housing," in Live in Hope, 2009, p.20.

12 Ibid.

13 Interview with Sr. Charlotte Davenport CSJP, 5-9-2025.

14 Davenport CSJP, 5-9-2025.

15 Ibid.

16 Lakefront Supportive Housing web site.

17 Mercy Housing Website blog, interview with Mark Angelini, Katie Cliff, 5-27-2024.

18 Mercy Housing Newsletter, Winter, 2014, p.7.

19 Mercy Housing Website, 9-1-2021.

20 Mercy Housing Press Release, October 29, 2015.

21 Ibid.

[22] Picot, Sister Rosalind, Letter to Ms. Brenda Ward, U.S. Department of Housing and Urban Development, 5-14-1999.

[23] Murphy, Sr. Lillian, "Allying Health Care and Housing." Reprinted from Health Progress, March-April 2005.

[24] "The Power of Collaboration", Strategic Healthcare Partnership progress report, 2002, p.1.

[25] Von, Hoffman, p. 19.

[26] Connecting Housing & Health. Strategic Healthcare Partnership Progress Report, 2003, p.3.

[27] 2008 Accountability Report for Ascension Health, August 2008, pp. 8-9.

[28] 2008 Accountability Report for Bon Seours Health System, August 2008, pp 5-6.

[29] "The Power of Collaboration," Strategic Healthcare Partnership progress report, 2002, p.10.

Chapter 6
[1] Inter-University Consortium Against Homelessness, excerpt from Ending Homelessness in Los Angeles, January 2007.

[2] Ibid.

[3] Ibid.

[4] Ibid.

[5] Mercy Housing Website blog, Recognizing Sister Diane: Shining a Light on her Dedication for Catholic Sisters Week, 3-13-2024

[6] Transcript of interview with Jack Burgis, 2007

[7] Interview with Sister Diane Clyne, 3-6-2024.

[8] Interview with Jane Graf, 10-4-2024.

[9] Transcript of interview with Jane Graf, 4-28-2021.

[10] Ibid.

[11] Mercy Housing Website, The Bigger the Challenge, the More I Like It: -- A Conversation with Jane Graf, 6-23-2020.

[12] Interview with Jane Graf, 3-5-2024.

[13] Burgis, 2007.

[14] Transcript of interview with Stan Keisling, 1-21-22.

[15] Mercy Housing Website, Celebrating 55 Years of Housing Justice with the Rural California Housing Corporation, 10-20-2024.

[16] *The Catholic Herald*, "Merger Forms Mercy Housing California", June17, 200, p.15.

[17] Website, National Rural Housing Coalition, "Housing Need in Rural America" June 2024.

[18] Ibid.

[19] Ibid.

[20] Sweat Equity refers to the work that potential house owners put into the building of their future home. Their labor reduces their costs.

[21] Mercy Housing Website, Celebrating 55 Years of Housing Justice with the Rural California Housing Corporation, October 20, 2024.

[22] Keisling, 4-20-2022.

[23] Graf, 4-20-2022.

[24] Ibid.

[25] Ibid.

[26] Ibid.

[27] Transcript of interview with Sister Amy Bayley, 4-20-2022.

[28] Margaret Talev, *LA Times*, "Rebirth of a Landmark", July 31, 1999.

[29] Strategic Healthcare Partnership: The Power of Collaboration, 2003, p.2.

[30] Mercy Housing Website, State Bill 4 Paves the Way for More Affordable Housing in California, 12-12-2023.

[31] Ibid.

[32] Mercy Housing, "News from our Neighborhoods", Fall, 2009, p.15.

[33] Bayley, April 20, 2022.

Chapter 7

[1] Mercy Housing Website, Impact

[2] Ten Principles for Developing Affordable Housing, The Urban Land Institute, 2007, p.1.

[3] Interview with Dara Kovel, 11-1-2024.

[4] Steven Spears, interview 9-7-24.

[5] Ten Principles for Developing Affordable Housing, The Urban Land Institute, 2007, p.2.

[6] Ibid.

[7] Interview with Dara Kovel, 11-1-2024.

[8]   Mercy Housing Website, Interview with Edna Jackson, 11-27-2018.

[9]   Transcript of interview with Sr. Geraldine Hoyer and Sr. Lillian Murphy, 3-24-2022.

[10]   Von Hoffman, Alexander, "The Transformation of Mercy Housing" in Live in Hope, 2011, p.26.

[11]   Ibid.

[12]   Ibid.

[13]   Ibid.

[14]   Ibid.

[15]   Reprinted from Health Progress, March-April 2005 Copyright © 2005 by The Catholic Health Association of the United State, pp 41-42.

[16]   Interview with Robin Haddock, 11-22-2024.

[17]   Ibid.

[18]   Mercy Housing Website blog, Savannah's History Lives On, 6-5-2024.

[19]   Mercy Housing Website blog, Rooted in History: Sweet Auburn Neighborhood Thrives, 2-2-2024.

[20]   Mercy Housing 2022 Impact Report.

[21]   Mercy Housing Website blog, Rooted in History: Sweet Auburn Neighborhood Thrives, February 2, 2024.

[22]   Pascal Sabino. "Landmark Sears Warehouse Wins Preservation Award After Being Converted To Affordable Housing", Block Club Chicago, September 9, 2019.

[23]   Ibid.

[24]   Ibid.

[25]   Interview with Mark Angelini, 11-22-2024.

[26]   Ibid.

[27]   Ibid.

[28]   Interview with Rich Ciraulo, 11-25-2024.

[29]   Affordable Tax Credit Coalition newsletter, 2020.

[30]   Ibid.

[31]   Ibid.

[32]   History.com Editors, The Great Recession, October 11, 2019.

[33]   Ibid.

[34]   Mercy Housing. News from Our Neighborhoods, Summer 2009, p.1.

[35]   Mercy Housing Website blog, Mercy Portfolio Services: Six Years of Community Impact 3-1-2016.

[36]   Jennifer Brown, Denver's first Native American affordable housing project aims to make amends for U.S. policy, *Colorado Sunday*, April 23, 2023.

[37]   Ibid.

[38]   Mercy Housing Website blog, Mercy Housing Selected to Provide Denver Metro Area's First Affordable Housing and Health Clinic Focused on Serving the American Indian and Alaska Native Community, 2-28-2023.

[39]   Mercy Housing Website blog, Modular Construction at Mercy Housing, 7-2-2019.

[40]   Mercy Housing. News from Our Neighborhoods, Fall, 2000, p.1.

[41]   Amelia Laing. Mercy Housing Website Blog, Mercy Housing Seeks to Make Affordable Housing Green through Environmental Initiative, Green Hope, 2-22-2016.

[42]   Mercy Housing Newsletter, Spring 2018, pp.1-2.

[43]   Leslie Fulbright, *San Francisco Chronicle*, Life at the bottom: S.F.'s Sunnydale project

Crumbling neighborhood, cut off from rest of the city, offers few avenues of escape, February 3, 2008.

[44]   Mercy Housing Website blog, The Bigger the Challenge, The More I Like It — A Conversation with Jane Graf, 6-23-2020.

[45]   San Francisco Planning Website, Sunnydale Hope SF, November 2024.

[46]   Mercy Housing Website blog, A Day to Celebrate! The Hub Opens its Doors to the Community, 10-17-2024.

Chapter 8

[1]   Tracy, Memo, January 1982.

[2]   Ibid.

[3]   Letter to Katherine Doyle, RSM from Ismael Guerrero, 2-3-2025.

[4]   Covert, Jennifer, Summation of Mercy Housing Success Plan, 4/16/2025

[5]   Lisa M. Schaffer, Esq., "Can Tenants Be Evicted for Domestic Violence?", Find Law website, March 21, 2019.

[6]   Mercy Housing Website blog, Homeless, Housed, Homeowner, Harvard, 1-3-2025.

[7]   Ibid.

8   Interview with Jacquie Hoffman, 1-9-2025.

9   Mercy Housing, Partnership Resource Guide and Agreement, pp.2, 14-19.

10   Interview with Jacquie Hoffman, January 9, 2025.

11   Mercy Housing Website, Green Hope.

12   Ibid.

13   Mercy Housing Partnership Resource Guide and Agreement, p.2.

14   Ibid.

15   Ibid. p. 1

16   Letter from Jacquie Hoffman to Sr. Katherine Doyle, RSM 2-18-2025.

17   Ibid. p.2.

18   Mercy Housing Annual Report, 2009, "Stability Changes Lives," p.10.

19   Ibid.

20   Ibid.

21   Mercy Housing Partnership Resource Guide and Agreement, p.5.

22   Mercy Housing, Annual Report 1998, "Diane Kock's Healthy Community," p.6.

23   Mercy Housing Website blog, "Residents Take the Lead in the Midwest," 3-22-2021.

24   Ibid.

25   Jane Graf, video message to Mercy Housing Personnel, April 1, 2020.

26   Jane Graf, letter to Mercy Housing Staff, 4-1-2020.

27   Mercy Housing Website blog, COVID-19 Response: Recovery and Resilience, 7-13-20.

28   Ibid.

29   Ibid.

30   USA Facts, Americans are struggling to afford enough food, 2-5-2024.

31   Ibid.

32   Mercy Housing Website blog, Pop-up Pantry Combats Seattle's Food Desert at Magnusom Park, 1-23-2020.

33   Mercy Housing Website blog, Collaboration Sees Success In Improving Nutrition in Affordable Housing Communities, 10-3-2024.

34   Mercy Housing Website blog, Collaboration Sees Success In Improving Nutrition in Affordable Housing Communities, 10-3-2024.

35 Mercy Housing, Strategic Healthcare Partnership Progress Report, 2003, Connecting Housing & Health, p.1.

36 Ibid.

37 Ibid.

38 Mercy Housing Annual Report 2004, p.11.

39 Mercy Housing Community Report, 2022, p.20.

40 Mercy Housing Website blog, Young Minds Become Entrepreneurs Through YouthBiz Program, 4-3-2024.

41 Mercy Housing Website blog, Do Resident Services Work? They Do-Take Sarah's Word for it!, 12-7-2022.

42 Connor, Beth. Case Study for Michael Boyd, 3-25-2025

43 Ibid.

44 Mercy Housing Website

45 Ismael Guerrero, Mercy Together: Our Differences Make the Difference! 4-22-2025.

46 Ibid

47 Mercy Housing Website

48 Mercy Housing Northwest Winter Newsletter, 2019.

49 Mercy Housing Website blog, Denver Metro Area's First Affordable Housing and Health Clinic Focused on Serving American Indian and Alaska Native Community, 2-28-2023.

50 Interview with Parag Gupta, 2-6-25.

51 Mercy Housing Annual Report, 2004, Respect, Justice and Mercy, p.7.

Chapter 9

1 Canon law is the set of laws which govern Church ministries. It sets down guidelines that Catholic institutions must follow such as devesting of property.

2 Sister Lillian Murphy, Memorandum, May 30, 2013, p.1.

3 Ibid., p.3.

4 Mercy Housing, "Coming to Completion Ceremony, Mercy Housing Corporate Member Group," December 2020.

5 Ibid.

6 USCCB, The Right to a Decent Home: #5-6.

7 Interview with Sister Jane Gerety RSM, 12-30- 2024.

8 Ibid.

9   Mercy Housing. Reflections on the Future of the Mercy Housing Ministry, 2017, p.14.

10   Leslie Fulbright, *San Francisco Chronicle*, "Life at the bottom: S.F.'s Sunnydale project Crumbling neighborhood, cut off from rest of the city, offers few avenues of escape," February 3, 2008.

11   Mercy Housing Website blog, The Bigger the Challenge, The More I Like It — A Conversation with Jane Graf, 6-23-2020.

12   Mercy Housing's Guiding Values, a reflection on Respect, Justice and Mercy, January 2020, p.14.

13   Mercy Housing Website, Leverage Milestone Reached, 10-22-2019.

14   Interview with Steve Spears, 9-7-24.

15   Mercy Housing Website, Interview with Edna Jackson, 2024.

16   Tracy, Memo, January 1982.

17   Interview with Patricia Cochran, 1-2-2025.

18   Mercy Housing Website. Who we serve/veterans.

19   Mercy Housing, 2016 annual report, p.9.

20   Mercy Housing California website, Boulevard Court, 2018.

21   Mercy Housing. Reflections on the Future of the Mercy Housing Ministry, 2017, p.13.

22   Ibid., p.14.

23   Interview with Sister Jane Gerety RSM, 12-30-2024.

24   Mercy Housing. Reflections on the Future of the Mercy Housing Ministry, 2017, p.13

25   Ibid., p.4.

26   Gerety, 12-30-2024.

27   Interview with Patricia Cochran, January 2, 2025.

28   Mercy Housing Community Matters Newsletter, 2024.

29   Cochran, pp.1-2, 2025.

www.ingramcontent.com/pod-product-compliance
Lightning Source LLC
Chambersburg PA
CBHW051251250726
48656CB00004B/1243